PIGEON SHOOTING

PIGEON SHOOTING

ARCHIE COATS

Edited by Colin Willock

ANDRE DEUTSCH

First published in 1963
This edition published July 1970
by André Deutsch Limited
105 Great Russell Street London wc1
Second Impression June 1973
Third Impression December 1975
Fourth Impression May 1978

Printed photolitho in Great Britain by
Ebenezer Baylis and Son Ltd
The Trinity Press, Worcester, and London

ISBN 0 233 96195 x

CONTENTS

I dedicated this book in 1963 to my dog Simba and his mother Juno. The best of companions on a lonely job, they have also saved me many hundreds of miles of walking!

APRIL 1969: *The line is still there, the line that keeps on picking up pigeons without tiring of them. Juno II is perhaps the best dog I have owned, and her daughter Locket already shows she has the right ideas.*

LIST OF ILLUSTRATIONS

INTRODUCTION

I have written this book for all pigeon shooters. For the young, who may well find that the wood pigeon will give them as much fun as they will ever get out of shooting game. And for the serious pigeon shooter, who will probably have to think of the financial side as I do. The combination of first-class sport with the destruction of a costly pest sounds attractive. But, as with everything else in life, there is a right and a wrong way to go about things. So I hope this book will help you all to obtain better sport and put more pigeons in the bag! But don't blame me if one day you find yourself half a mile from your car, with 150 wet pigeons to carry across three very soggy ploughed fields!

My thanks are due to Colin Willock, who has patiently listened to my protestations; to the Ministry of Agriculture, Fisheries and Food for permission to quote from their Advisory Booklets; to the *Shooting Times* for permission to use material mostly contained in the chapter 'Advanced Decoying', and for various photographs, taken by Gordon Carlisle; to the Federation of Rabbit Clearance Societies Ltd, for permission to use material contained in their Newsletters; to John Tarlton for permission to use photographs; to Dr R. K. Murton of the Ministry of Agriculture Field Research Station; and to Stella Hipkins, who typed the book.

I would also like to pay tribute to the countrymen I

meet. First, the gamekeepers: if there ever was a dedicated job, surely this is it, especially nowadays when modern farming makes life so hard for them and their charges. For those who rely on many tame birds, it is not so bad. But for those who look after wild birds, protecting and feeding them regularly all the year round, only to find that 80 per cent of their successfully hatched young almost immediately die of starvation, it is pretty trying. Then there are those who work on the land. The agricultural wage is better than it was, but still they could get more in a factory. But they stay on the land which claims them as it claims the keeper. Me too. It is a way of life and I do not regret it.

In preparing a new edition of this book I have made few changes. At the end of some of the sections I have added comments or suggestions which reflect my experience over the six years since the book was first published.

In April 1969, I still have no regrets about my choice of livelihood as a professional pigeon shooter. You may not get very rich but it is better than the commuter's train. But until farmers are ready to look on a full-time pigeon shooter as they would a vet, or as a form of insurance in defence of their own crops, I could not advise the many people who have asked me about my job to actually take up pigeon shooting as a profession.

THE RING-NECKED DOVE

That naughty bird *Columba palumbus*, the ring-necked dove or wood pigeon, is indeed a bad boy and does a vast amount of harm to all members of the farming fraternity. He will also eat all the green stuff in your back garden as a side line. Nevertheless, I am very fond of him, though I make my living out of his destruction.

No one seems to know exactly when the pigeon was first heard of or mentioned in the United Kingdom. Certainly the Romans ate pigeons, and considered them a delicacy, but whether they imported them, as they did the pheasant, no one has recorded. It is hard to say whether the pigeons depicted on certain fifteenth-century murals in the British Museum are *Columba palumbus* or not. Anyway, the wood pigeon now lives and breeds all over this country, wherever conditions are suitable and sometimes when they are not.

The 'woody' makes a rather flat and flimsy nest of enlaced twigs in any thickish bush or tree, though usually not more than twenty feet from the ground. Several old books I have read state that he makes his nest well up. With this I must respectfully disagree. Perhaps he did so when our forests were well kept and there was not the present enticing habitat of secondary growth and mixed forestry plantations. There are two white eggs, laid any time as soon as the weather permits the birds to pair off. But nature, with the help of various predatory creatures who pinch the eggs, sees to it that very few young pigeons fly before the middle of August. Hence the present Rabbit Clearance Society Pigeon Poking Programme, which should cover the area twice at six-weekly intervals, the last week of July and the first week of August and the second and third week of September respectively. Old birds are tending more and more to lay later in the year, if their nests have been thus poked. Perhaps they will learn to lay camouflaged eggs, or lay them in holes like their ancestors!

Incubation lasts about seventeen days, both birds sitting, though one will carry on if the other is killed. I have often wondered, though I have no proof, if a foster parent does not possibly take over the incubation, or at least the feeding of the young, if both the original parents are killed. Though very necessary, it is unpleasant to shoot parent pigeons coming in to laid wheat in July or August, knowing that there are probably squabs in the nest.

I have shot the same flock of pigeons in the same field, several times. These often came from mixed forestry blocks, where the nests are liable to be very close together especially when the deciduous trees acquire their leaves. Though the pairs were always being broken up, yet there seemed to be young flying in September from the same area. You do not find many dead squabs under the trees or in the nest. It is rather odd unless the survivors raise the orphaned young.

The young stay in the nest for about three weeks and are fed by the regurgitation of a milky fluid from either parent's crop. They put their beaks down the parent's throat, the young beak being soft and shovel-like at this period. This food, mostly partly digested grain at this time, is full of protein which may be one of the reasons why more squabs survive at this period than earlier on, when their parents are eating young kale or other less nutritive food. No one can say that the young look very pretty. Naked to start with, and then with a scant covering of down, they quickly grow and are flying in about six weeks. Accompanied at the beginning by one or both parents, they soon learn the form and greedily cram their own crops with someone's wheat or barley.

The Migration Problem

But these are the early ones: the main body of young-sters do not fly until late August or September, by which time the harvest is probably over. Towards the end of September and particularly in October, the young birds flock together and move about the country gleaning from the stubbles. Then, perhaps by way of a one-year ley, they learn that clover tastes good too. These packs of first-year birds provide, I think, the basis for all stories of thousands of migratory birds ('they furriners') who visit these shores. Certainly the tendency is for movement down the East Coast and probably sometimes over the sea. People say 'Oh, these birds are smaller and darker.' Indeed they are, as being juveniles, they have yet to grow their white ring!

If they are not birds bred in this country, where do they come from? The vast forests of Scandinavia? I have been into this fairly carefully over a number of years. Corres-pondents from Sweden and Norway tell me that there are a few pigeons in the south, but 'we wish there were more to shoot'. In Denmark, and Holland as well, farmers are encouraged by grants to shoot pigeons only over a certain period of the year. And they too would be glad of more chances to shoot them. It is a fact that the woodland in all continental countries is usually better kept than ours. Also, these northern countries grow large areas of black firs which makes me doubt that there can be a large number of resident pigeons. Pigeons do not like solid blocks of black firs to nest or live in, and usually use only fifty or sixty yards from the edge, and that only when they are near cultivation.

There are more pigeons in Belgium and the north of France, but nothing like the resident population of this country. I once killed 42 *Pigeons Ramier* on clover on a by-day, while shooting near Laon in the Aisne. My hide was a Kaiser war shell-hole. This was considered quite a feat and duly noted in the local press. But nobody goes out seriously to shoot pigeons and nothing else. Don't forget that shooting is very popular in France, though there are relatively few keepered shoots. So game is scarce and if there were any pigeons the local sportsmen would certainly go for them. Incentive? Pigeons cost around 7s 6d in Paris and are rightly esteemed for the table! Shades of the Common Market!

Most of these continental birds migrate south, if they migrate at all, through certain passes in the Western Pyrenees into Spain. There, during the *Passage*, as they call it, quite a number are shot, or trapped, usually with the help of live decoys. It is quite an event. The local *Guardas* watch the known flight lines, and as soon as the first arrivals appear, the wires hum. I am told that it is notoriously difficult to do any official business, at the highest level, during the *Passage*! The same hides, built on the mountainside and commanding the lines of flight are used every year, and the live decoys, tethered on a convenient tree, are simply 'lifted' at the appropriate moment, to show the weary travellers the way to a good resting place. This may well be their last, as the standard of shooting in Spain is pretty high.

Other species

The 'Woody', as he is called here, goes by other names elsewhere. Most of them are unprintable, but we used to call pigeons 'Cushat' or 'Cushy Doo', or simply 'Doo' in my native Ayrshire. The Welsh call them 'Queest' or 'Quist'. I remember giving a pigeon lecture once, in Led-bury, I think, and a chap got up almost as soon as I had started and said, 'Can I ask a question?' Other lecturers will understand when I said 'Yes' rather unwillingly, and he said, 'What is the difference between a Quist and a wood pigeon?' I answered 'None', and he at once replied, 'Thank you very much. That's what I came for, I'll now——off!'

We have three other wild resident pigeons or doves in the United Kingdom. The first, the stock dove, is descended from the cage birds kept for culinary uses by the monks. I agree with them that stock doves are better eating than the ring-neck, particularly in winter. They always look fat and healthy and seem to be able to find corn or seeds even in the depth of winter, when the poor old woody is looking very sorry for himself, getting rid of your kale almost as quickly as he eats it. The stock dove eats little green stuff and is particularly fond of seeds, and not only weed seeds, I regret to say. With a lovely iridescent green and purple neck and upper breast, he is much smaller than the wood pigeon. Alas, the market values them according to size and usually classifies him as 'small'. Usually rather wary, he can be stupid enough on occasions. If you shoot one, its mate is liable to come in again, which is rather pathetic and makes one wonder if they mate for life. They also carry more shot than any bird I know, though this may be because they are small enough to go through anything but the centre of a pattern. Otherwise, their habits as far as decoying is concerned are much the same as the wood pigeons. They will come into wood pigeon decoys.

The almost indentical rock dove, often a slightly lighter colour, is, on the other hand, a bird of the wild coasts and cliffs. They never sit in trees. I have seen them on the stooked oats in Islay, and no doubt you could decoy them, but I was on holiday and I could not have cared at the time if I never saw another pigeon! They make wonderful shooting if you can get on the line of flight back to the caves where they live, or go in a boat, if you are a good sailor. The boatman fires a ·22 into the cave and they simply whizz out, making very difficult snap-shooting. I can assure you there is no time to fire your first barrel, be sick and then fire the second. I know!

The collared dove, which has recently established itself as a breeding resident, has not reached pest proportions—yet!

The turtle dove, a migrant who comes here to nest, is on the protected list and is a charming little bird who really does little harm, except maybe eating a little grain now and then. He has a collar of black feathers with white tips round the top of his breast and front of the neck, and the feathers of his slightly fan tail are tipped with white too. I remember liberating some in Benghazi in 1941. I was buying vegetables in the local 'souk', still operating no matter in whose hands the town was at the moment. There were about five cages full of these wretched birds, caught, like the quail, exhausted on migration. Suddenly the siren went, heralding the Stukas. Needless to say the local inhabitants departed as a man to the cellars, so I opened the cages and let the doves out, hoping that blast might be blamed as the culprit. Actually no bombs were dropped, but we were too far away in the truck by then to hear the lamentations.

WHY DO WE HAVE SO MANY
PIGEONS?

Historical

I don't for a moment suggest that there is no migration into or out of this country. I have no doubt there is some, but I believe, and I think this is now the official view, that 85 per cent of the so-called 'foreigners' are locally bred. Other countries simply do not possess the stock, or suitable habitat conditions to produce them. Why then do we have so many pigeons? Blame the Kaiser, that convenient whipping boy. Before the First World War, there were plenty of pigeons. And no doubt they were a menace, but nothing like on the scale they are now. They also ate a lot of weed seeds. *British Sporting Birds*, by F. B. Kirkman and Horace G. Hutchinson cites an example given by St John in his delightful *Wild Life in the Highlands*: 'He wished to prove to a farmer that a large flock of wood pigeons, busily at work in a field of young clover, were really his benefactors. To prove this point he shot eight from the field which was being ravaged, and in the presence of the farmer, straight away opened their crops. The results were exactly in accordance with his predictions. The birds had not been eating the clover but every pigeons' crop was as full as it could possibly be of the seeds of the worst weeds in the country, the wild mustard and the ragweed which they had found remaining on the surface of the ground. Indeed, during the whole of the summer

B

and the spring all pigeons must feed entirely on the seeds
of different wild plants.'

But during the 1914–18 war, much of the country's best
timber was cut down. The secondary growth that succeeded it provided (and still does) perfect nesting cover.
Then came the Forestry Commission, and the next war
and more cutting. Where large blocks of pure conifers have
been planted, you will only find pigeons nesting or roosting on the fringes. With the mixed plantation now
favoured by the Forestry Commission, principally beech or
other hardwood and conifers, the pigeon has the perfect
home all the way through the block and all the year round.
It is not too thick to get into to nest, but thick enough for
some protection from his enemies and warm as a winter roost.

Then we needed, in both wars, to survive the U-boat
menace and so had to grow more food. This led to a more
modern concept of farming with the idea of producing more
and more food per acre. The result has been that the weeds
are gone and there are many thousands more acres under
the plough. I fear that St John would not find many
pigeons' crops full of weed seeds today. A notable
example of the unexpected effect of this process took place
this year. At the time of writing, 25th May, 1962, I always
used to shoot pigeons on charlock coming up in the young
corn. Granted for once they were doing good, but it was
an easy way of getting rid of the local population before
they tackled something more valuable. Spraying has
ensured that very little charlock survives in this area. So
the pigeons simply remain on clover until young kale or
grass comes up. Then they may get some charlock as at
present it is dangerous to spray the young crop until it is
able to stand it. But they may have solved this problem
by the time you read this! And so it goes on.

Now the normal farm rotation gives the pigeon something to eat all the year round in all weathers except in prolonged snow and ice conditions. All over this part of the country (Hampshire and Berkshire) much of the downland has come under the plough and there are acres of clover and cereals, with plenty of nice cattle troughs to supply the water the pigeon must have.

At the end of the last war there were fewer pigeons. The price provided an incentive to shoot them, and the Government provided cheap cartridges. How much was this also due to a shortage of keepers who had been to the wars? Were there not more predators about to eat the eggs and the young? This is perfectly true and must have had an effect, though I would not for one minute consider advising anyone to produce jays or magpies specifically to keep the pigeon population in bounds! The grey squirrel also eats pigeons' eggs, but his presence in a forestry block is also undesirable. You cannot have it both ways.

Dr R. K. Murton of the Ministry of Agriculture's Research Station, Worplesdon, is the great authority on the ecology of wood pigeons. Those interested must read *The Breeding of Wood Pigeon Populations*, *The Autumn Migration of Wood Pigeon* and *Some Survival Estimates for the Wood Pigeon*. All three are reprinted from his classic work *Birdstudy*. Dr Murton estimates the wood pigeon population in UK at 'not less than five million and not more than ten million'. He also states that under normal breeding conditions, if you have 2,000 adults in July, by the end of the breeding season, which probably means the end of October, you are likely to have 2,000 young as well. So you can see that it is really quite a problem.

Habitat

I have already mentioned that modern forestry practice favours the wood pigeon both as regards nesting and roosting cover. Otherwise he prefers strips, parkland and small spinneys, to the dense mass of great woods. Personally I think this is because he is a lazy creature and likes his home to be pretty close to his restaurant, so that he can fly to his chosen field without much bother. Nevertheless, he definitely prefers to feed in an open space. So the downland country, with its belts and strips is often the best game country and also harbours most pigeons. There is always what I call good 'background' to a favourite pigeon area. By this I mean a number of woods or belts which provide roosting or nesting cover in season and which he uses as a base. And he must have water, whether it be a pond or a stream or merely, as in the case of the downs, a generous supply of cattle drinking troughs.

With a little practice you can 'read' a one-inch map and can soon spot the likely areas. The contour line plays a part as it may determine the line of flight. Pigeons do not normally fly across a height of land, they fly along it. Thus they will follow a wooded ridge, rarely cross it. The same thing applies to salient features on the ground. They use strips to fly down or along. They will use a gap in that strip to fly through, particularly in wind. They may pick a small clump of trees as a staging post or resting place, on their way to and from their field. They rarely fly without a purpose and that purpose is almost always the gratification of their desire to be gregarious, to eat together in one chosen field. Though pigeons move about the country from about the middle of October until the end of April, they are nevertheless parochially minded once they settle down. They may come to you from some distance away, but once they decide your crops are to their liking and they are not frozen to death at night, then they will stick around and won't go away until the food gives out, is better on your neighbour's land, or you make things too hot for them. The only time your locals, particularly the young, will leave you is in October. The bad time to have a visitation is about the end of March. If the weather is mild and the clover good, or you are spring sowing, it is highly probable that they will be with you for the duration, so to speak.

About the middle of February last year, I shot a one-year ley for the third or fourth time and killed about 60. There were not many left I thought smugly. Nor were there three days later, when I happened to be with the Agent. Full marks to Coats! But then there was a gale and soon after the phone rang and a well-known voice said, 'You had better have a look at that one-year ley again.' I did, next day. 165. And this often happens. But at least I was there. These 165 were shot on a Monday. No 'Sorry can't come till next weekend' in this case.

There is an interesting publication called *The Wood Pigeon in Great Britain* by M. K. Colquhoun. This Agricultural Research Council report, series no. 10, is obtainable from H.M. Stationery Office at 3s. It gives much useful information on pigeons' habits, but I must say I do not agree with every word in it. To sum up, their seasonal habitat is determined largely by the food supply and they often live quite close to it!

Pigeon Damage

Pigeon damage in this country is wellnigh incalculable An attempt has been made by my friends at the Kynoch Game Advisory Service at Fordingbridge to assess the cost. All that one can say is that it comes to many millions of pounds. The Ministry of Agriculture and Fisheries now say that pigeon damage is as much as the rabbit did before myxomatosis. As he apparently stuffed himself to the tune of fifty million pounds a year, the pigeon is obviously doing himself nicely. About 550 tons of human or animal food are eaten in the south of England area alone per day.

I have worked out the following figures which will be of interest to the layman, and indeed to those farmers who are hesitant about joining a Rabbit Clearance Society or otherwise getting their pigeons dealt with. I don't for a moment say they are dead accurate, but I doubt if they are very far out.

A pigeon will eat up to 1,000 to 1,300 grains of wheat a day. In July or August this would be about one and a half cropfuls. A cropful weighs up to three and a half ounces. So let us say, five ounces a day. It takes thirty ounces of wheat to make a $1\frac{1}{2}$ lb loaf of white bread. Therefore a pigeon eats the equivalent in six days.

A pigeon will eat 800 to 1,000 grains of malting quality barley in a day. Barley swells more than wheat, but the birds will still get through one and a half cropfuls in summer which weigh about three to four ounces. It takes three ounces of malting quality to make 1·18 pints of mild ale. Therefore the thirsty and envious will note that a pigeon can live, like the Latuka tribesmen in Equatorial Sudan, in an alcoholic stupor for most of the summer months. Foolish birds, they prefer wheat! Incidentally, from these figures I now realize why my brewing friends always seem to have the odd Rolls-Bentley around!

Say a farmer ploughs, harrows and then plants ten acres of kale. Total cost in labour and seed might be £125. He loses the crop through pigeon damage and has to resow. If the crop comes a second time he is further out of pocket to the tune of about £25. But maybe there is a drought and the second crop fails, even though the pigeons have nothing to do with it. Then he loses the lot and in addition he may have to buy in nuts or sugar beet as winter feed for his cattle to replace the lost kale. All this may cost £250. And no doubt the keeper or shooting tenant will be sore at the loss of a good pheasant stand. On the other side of the boundary, Coats has been on the job. As a result a fine crop of kale stands ready to receive the boundary birds and maybe some of your tame ones too! Think well, ye game preservers! In snow, unprotected kale will assuredly be stripped or rendered unpalatable by pigeon droppings and here again extra food may have to be provided.

Pigeons are gourmets as well as gourmands. They eat the best of the clover, particularly on a one-year ley. Permanent pastures also get badly hit, though they may get away with it if on a large scale. Packed absolutely tight in the crop, three to four ounces of your clover may not seem a great weight, but shake the crop out on a dinner plate and you will be surprised at the volume. And each leaf is a good leaf, right from where it hurts the plant most. And do not forget that they digest it continually as they eat, as the droppings on your sward will show. Protein is the most expensive part of a cow's diet, so you might as well grow as much of it as you can on your own swards instead of buying it. Clover has about 25 per cent of dry matter protein, whereas grass has up to 20 per cent. Clover produces nitrogen from the air; grass needs nitrogen, so if the pigeons take the clover you may have a nice little bill for artificial nitrogen. Nowadays sheep seem to be kept more on clover and the modern tendency is away from folding on swedes, rape, etc. How much this is due to the pigeons, which will eat rape at any season and take it in preference to clover, I do not know. Hardy clovers are good for pigs. I killed my record bag on S.100 Aberystwyth.

Lucerne is another crop which they will sadly deplete in its young stage in June, in winter and especially when the new leaf shoots in the spring.

Many people simply won't grow peas, as the pigeons are liable to get the lot, when sown and later in the pod. Some time ago, I was asked to go to a big estate in Essex where they grow 900 acres of canning peas. I could only advise them to have a permanent pigeon shooter. This they have done, with good results, though of course the pigeons are kept down at all times and wherever they concentrate, and not only on the peas.

The seed growers suffer much. A plant must be in good heart to produce quality seed. Crops grown for seed provide the epicurean pigeon with the best there is. Steady and timely shooting on the crop itself is without doubt the best way of saving it. I have had a terrible time this year with seed rape, six fields of it. At least the farmers will get a good crop now, but I and a helper or two shot 23 days in June and 14 in July before the fields were safe. We killed 1,650 pigeons. I often shot three fields in a day and was in action up to 7.30 pm.

There is a certain amount of seed grass grown around here. This is mostly S.23 and 24 Rye grass and S.53 fescue. They are worth from 1s to 3s a pound to the grower. This year a certain farmer had a large field of perhaps forty acres. Pigeons really set into it, as they do when it goes flat before combining and at one time I thought there were at least 1,000 on it. I weighed the crops of several shot coming home from the field the evening before I decoyed it. The average came to about three ounces. Say these 1,000 birds were there for a week (and they were probably there longer) and ate six ounces or two cropfuls in a day. If you think this is too much, remember the damage done by 'shedding' with their great feet. So the farmer lost 375 lb a day at an average price of 2s per pound which comes to £37 10s a day, or £262 10s in a week, as pigeons do not knock off for the weekend. I shot this field to give a friend a good shoot and because the farm borders ground which I look after. But no cartridges for me or anyone else. How stupid can you get? This is bad neighbour policy as well, as he is a member of the local Rabbit Clearance Society.

Market gardeners know all too well what fate their brassicas will suffer, when young, and again when the snow comes. Early this year the Brussel sprout growers in East Anglia took a pretty good pasting, and the possible loss can be worked out on the two examples given. In both cases what the pigeons do not eat they probably ruin by their droppings. Cost of growing winter cabbage including labour, fertilizer, seed, spraying, etc., may come to £35 an acre. Harvesting or cutting accounts for another £15, and so a total of £50. Your eventual return might average £80. The cost of growing sprouts or broccoli will be about £50 an acre and the cost of harvesting, £30. On an outlay of £80 your average return might be £120 an acre, though in both these cases these figures can fluctuate considerably.

The foregoing was written in 1963; costs nowadays are obviously much higher. Now that the subsidy is off barley, there is a growing tendency to plant beans, peas, and various seed crops all of which delight the pigeons gastronomic juices. But all these crops are vulnerable to pigeon damage which is liable to be financially painful.

Much more winter wheat is planted and this had made life more difficult in July. Whereas there were probably only one or two fields of winter wheat on a farm, in this area, there are now several, so the choice of the pigeon is that much greater.

Any village, and indeed suburban, garden, can be ruined by pigeons, especially in winter. My own is no exception, and this year we have no cabbages and what was left of the broccoli was not fit to eat. You can laugh if you like!

I show a pigeon diet sheet at the end of this chapter. This shows the normal menu taken month by month as the farming calendar rotates its even round. It refers mainly to this part of the world, but local choices are easy to add. For instance, East Anglian pigeons are very fond of old potatoes in the Fen areas in the autumn.

Perhaps I should mention bangers and carbide guns. They work for a bit, and the carbide guns are good for small fields and will certainly do their jobs. But none of these things KILL pigeons, and I consider them unneighbourly weapons, at least in areas where shooting is possible. For the small garden 'Scaraweb Nylon Floss' seems a good answer. It seems rather expensive, but if carefully used and teased out it covers a lot of ground, and does the trick.

What good do pigeons do? I have already said that this year's spraying has seen charlock virtually on the way out. They do eat chickweed and are very fond of it. Most farmers are loath to admit that they have chickweed on the farm, but if you see a crop of corn about 4 in high and there is no easily identifiable yellow charlock, but pigeons are settling in the field, the chances are that they are after chickweed and will give you a good shoot. I have found small snails in them, but doubt if these were harmful to agriculture. You do find the odd weed seed but rarely a cropful. I would be only too happy if someone could tell me a point in their gastronomic favour. In due season they eat wild strawberries and blackberries, though you usually find these mixed with their normal ration. In winter, haws, ivy berries, and various other oddments are included in their diet.

Farmers should rejoice when there is a great beech-mast or acorn year, for then the pigeons' attention is diverted from the farm for as long as the woods provide them with sustenance. Here again, though, they often mix the nuts with a liberal ration of clover. But such years may provide only a temporary respite, as I have an idea that when we do get any number of migrants from overseas, the draw is the large nut crop. How they know that the nuts are there is beyond me, and perhaps one imagines that the con- centrations are large, because they are often in places where pigeons are not normally much in evidence. Those who wish to grow beeches should use the mast from the crops of the slain. I tried this out, rather sceptically, but now have some fine young beeches, a much higher average 'hatch' than usual. I have tried it out with acorns and they certainly grow when planted straight from a pigeon's crop, but I doubt if the germination is any better.

I normally take a holiday in late April or May as pigeons are very keen on beech and other buds and are impossible to get at, hardly leaving the trees all day. This is one case where I cannot believe that any one tree's buds taste better than the others. Anyway, it works out very well for me, as this period coincides nicely with the fishing! But, of

WOOD PIGEONS

WHAT THEY EAT AND WHEN THEY EAT IT

This applies to the Southern Counties. Diets vary elsewhere

Month	Weather	Main Diet	and	Second Choice	Remarks
January	Mild	Clover		Rape — Lucerne	Usually white clover pasture or 1st-year ley. You can't decoy on snow
	Hard	Kale or any green crop showing above snow		Haw or ivy berries	
February	Mild	Clover		Rape — Lucerne	Roosting time and decoying outside the wood
	Hard	As for January, but they will go back to clover at the least sign of thaw			
March	Normal	Clover until spring sowing begins			They feed between showers
April	Normal	Spring sowing, then back to clover		Any beans and peas are a certain draw	Preference is for wheat but depends on locality
May	Normal	Clover or beech buds to start with, then anything young like kale or mustard, rape including charlock or clover			Usually permanent ley, if clover
June	Normal	Charlock, chickweed, young kale, mustard and rape, or well eaten down clover		Lucerne	After dawn feeding does not start again much before midday

July	Normal	Young kale or mustard and charlock, then any corn which ripens and is then laid. Grass seed	Preference for wheat, usually winter sown in 'milky' stage
August	Normal	Laid corn. Again preference for wheat, then stubbling after harvest. Watch beans	Some young birds flying. Watch whatever water is available. Grain makes them thirsty
September	Normal	Stubbling. A gradual changeover from wheat to barley	Most young birds on the wing
October	Normal	Depends on the weather and the ploughing. A gradual changeover from barley stubbling to clover, beech-mast or acorns in season	Often on stubble undersown as a 1st-year ley
November	Mild	Clover or grain until blackened by frost	Green crops	Often difficult to get at in a 'game' country
	Hard	Beech-mast or acorns, depending on the weather. Clover where possible		
December	Mild	Clover or Lucerne	Pigeon get 'poor'
	Hard	Any green crops above snow	

course, there are exceptional years. The 1962–3 winter completely upset normal pigeon routine. The snow refrigerated the old barley and in March the survivors were still eating it, hardly touching clover.

PRELIMINARIES

Getting Permission

I get many letters from people asking me how they can find pigeon shooting. Some of them sound rather bitter, and indeed many of the 'Letters to the Editor' which one reads in the sporting press have obviously been written by individuals who have not had much luck in their quest for shooting.

To start with, people should understand the law, though the law is not easy to understand in that there is little definitely written specifically as regards pigeons. You cannot just go and shoot pigeons as a right, even if they are pests on the unprotected list. You require a shotgun permit, though not a game licence. Taken from the top down, the landlord or owner, his guests or nominees have first right if the land-owner has the shooting. This might include his agent. If the landlord shoots pigeons to any tenant farmer's satisfaction, that tenant will not exercise his right to nominate 'a man with a gun' if he does not wish to shoot himself. Otherwise he can do so. And this is generally held valid for pigeons, though in fact there is no mention of pigeons in the Act which is meant to cover ground game. But the shooting tenant, if there is one, takes priority over the farming tenant (and the owner too, I think, though I cannot get a definite answer on this and am prepared to be shot down over it!). This is provided the shooting tenant does the job satisfactorily, otherwise the tenant can complain to the owner and in the last resort to the local Pest Officer, who, through the Ministry, may serve notice in writing, under Section 98(1) of the 1947 Agricultural Act, usually on the owner/occupier 'requiring him to take steps'. Thank Heavens these powers are rarely enforced. Finally, the keeper has probably the most powerful say of all, and if he wants to shoot the pigeons, you've had it.

All this sounds complicated, and indeed it is complicated. On the face of it, you would fairly reason, 'the pigeons need killing, why don't they let me do it?' The answer is, people are chary, and rightly so, of letting strangers on their land, and with guns at that. Maybe there have not been many instances of pigeon shooters abusing their privileges, but there *have* been some, and word has got around and a better-safe-than-sorry view taken.

When I started this job, I had to go very slowly and often missed many a good shoot, because I could not get around some link in the chain of command. The longest list I can think of, from the bottom up, is farmer — beat keeper — head keeper — agent — shooting tenant or owner. See the farmer first, having spotted the field in which the pigeons are feeding. Later in this chapter I have explained how to do this. He will probably say he will be delighted, but 'you had better see the keeper'. So you set off to find the keeper, who is sure to be out, and his wife will know nothing, experience having taught her that this is by far the safest answer! So you are up a gum tree and the one thing *not* to do is go ahead and shoot on the 'I didn't think it would matter' or 'I thought it would be all right' basis. When you eventually see the keeper, tell him you've seen Mr X, the farmer, who would like you to shoot pigeons on Y field. Be specific as to its locality. Say that

Mr X suggested that you should see him, the keeper. This may do the trick, though any other local references may increase your chances a lot. To be able to say, 'I killed 26 off Mr Jones's laid wheat at Howe Farm last Saturday' can do no harm. But you may still be referred up the chain from beat keeper to head keeper and so on. And you must play it that way; in the long run it pays. What you eventually want, at least as a start, is to be given a position as some sort of unofficial pigeon shooter over a farm or estate. Use that position as you value it. Always ask the keeper, make it a strict rule. Out of season, you may get to know him well enough to leave a message in his house with his wife. But if he is at the other end of his beat, perhaps watching for a stoat to show, he will be understandably peeved if he hears shots and has to investigate. Do not let your recreation interfere with his job.

I have written elsewhere that pigeon decoying in a static hide does not disturb or harm game in any way. Birds will feed quite happily in the same field, and will only look up, or maybe run into the hedge, when you leave the hide to pick up, but they are soon out again. Walking about and banging away up hedgerows is an entirely different matter and keepers will quite rightly object.

During the nesting season, the pigeon decoyer must be very careful, when siting his hide, to avoid nests. If I have to use the hedgerows, I ask the keeper if he knows of a nest by such and such a tree or wherever it is I want to make the hide. But I always look carefully anyway, twenty feet each way, before starting operations. Once you are installed, you act as a literal and, we hope, lethal, scarecrow, and indeed I often put out a rook or crow as a decoy with the pigeons. Your hide will often be in the open ground, where rooks do as much damage as crows, so you keep that area clear of them at least for the day. I must admit that when nesting is in full swing, I try to get bale hides put out. Then I know I can do nothing but good. Anyway the crops that I am protecting are valuable, and I reason that the farmer can take a little trouble to provide bales, while I protect the sitting birds!

I think that more and more keepers realize that a stationary and reliable gun on their beat is in their interest, and that you are partly doing their job for them. But if they are happy for you to shoot pigeons, then you must watch their interests in other directions. No one expects to shoot pigeons immediately before a shoot, but it is quite possible for the interested trilogy to work together. This comprises Farmer Jones, who wants the pigeons shot, the keeper who wants his game undisturbed and yet wants to keep in with Farmer Jones (hoping for that field of roots on the boundary next year), and the poor pigeon shooter who gets it all ways.

Scene — A telephone conversation

AGENT OR FARM MANAGER: The pigeons are murdering the rape for the sheep in the 20-acre.

COATS: I'll see the keeper.

COATS (*later*): He says they are shooting next week and that field is a stand.

AGENT OR F M: By that time there won't be any rape left for the sheep *or* the pheasants.

COATS (*hopefully, with visions of a 100-day*): Well — you're the boss.

AGENT OR F M: No dice, you know as well as I do that HE would never stand for it.

COATS: Yes.

Scene ends

So find out the shooting dates and arrange with the keeper or shooting tenant to keep the ground quiet. They will appreciate this and you will benefit in the long run. On the other hand, I have been asked to shoot on a boundary or at the end of a long strip leading to the boundary, on shooting days, to act as a stop and keep straying birds back where they belong!

Perhaps the other outstanding point to clarify with the keeper is whether you may take a dog. Frankly, I always take Simba, but he is pretty good at this job, and trained to it, and I only use him to pick up birds on their backs or runners in the open. When I see a bird fall at the edge of a hedge or a tree, I make him sit in the hide, when I pick up at the end, and go and get it myself. In the nesting season, to avoid nest disturbance, I just leave them. Even in out-of-season days, I only let him hunt the hedgerows near the hide for runners and I think you would be well advised to copy this. It all adds up to good relations between you and the keeper and, believe me, these are terribly important to your future as a pigeon shooter.

So this is the best way to get permission: *on* the ground, *with* the actual individuals concerned. Do not write, do not telephone but come and see them with an actual proposition: 'The pigeons are there. Can I shoot them?' And if possible, come armed with some reference. To start with, and I say this bluntly, pigeon shooting is best done on your own. Only when you get to know the individuals well enough, can you ask permission to 'bring a friend'. Perhaps it does not matter so much if you both occupy the same hide, but you had better specify this.

Becoming a member of a pigeon shooting-cum-wildfowling club may be the next best chance of getting shooting on private estates, the secretary having presumably contacted them and arranged that members of the club may shoot pigeons or other vermin, perhaps with RCS or club cartridges. Being an experienced 'shot' (or being on the local RCS or Pest Officer's list as such), covers a multitude of sins and I know one or two on the local list who have yet to fire a gun! I think it is all wrong that merely to be a member of a RCS should automatically entail being accorded the status of an expert or experienced shot. I do not believe that it was ever the Ministry's intention when they first started the cartridge scheme that this should be the case, but I fear it is, and it leads to abuse in much the same way as the old free-cartridge scheme. At least I know one committee member of a local RCS who went to the gun-maker supplying the cartridges and said, 'Can I have my allotment, please. We are shooting tomorrow.' And I don't think he was talking of pigeons! But, being an experienced shot gives you a reference and entitles you to obtain cartridges from RCS members, which is another good reason for getting on the list! But when you first start, you must weigh up the form rather carefully. The farmer may be delighted to let you shoot his pigeons, but he may baulk at giving you, or even selling you, RCS cartridges at reduced prices. Farmers are funny that way and you may be wise not to broach the subject until you have a reasonable bag to confront him with; 'I think I've saved your young kale for the moment, any chance of some cartridges next time?' It is really a question of weighing your pleasure in shooting against the cost. Farmers are inclined to look on pigeon shooting as a favour. Indeed it is, and most people are only too pleased to get it and forget the cost. But that does not make it any less right that the farmer should be willing to pay something towards the protection of his crops, particularly if someone is willing to come regularly. I must admit that I do not shoot pigeons anywhere now unless I get help financially or in cartridges. It is my job and I simply can't afford it otherwise. Alas, the day has long since gone when one could make pigeon shooting pay, just by shooting and selling them. One has to be retained as well. My last job in the Army, before being demobbed, was as Instructor at Sandhurst. When I could get weekends off, I used to come down to Basingstoke in my Austin 7 (I can't remember too well where I got the petrol!) and stay in an hotel. If I shot 100 pigeons during my stay, I paid for that petrol, the hotel, cartridges, etc, and put £15 in my pocket. It was fun while it lasted.

Little by little, when you play your cards properly, you will slowly build up a clientèle, the open sesame being not only the results achieved, but the way you go about it. The local grapevine will then sound the all clear. Whichever way you get permission, by your efforts, or through a club or RCS, you can make or mar the future by your actions. I repeat: make certain whom you are to inform when you intend to come. If it is the keeper, come to some definite agreement with him on that score. Don't leave gates open — don't cut down or hack about good timber to make hides — leave your hides clean — remove waste paper even if you leave the cartridge cases, but remove them, too, if there is any chance of stock eating them. Shoot vermin and hang it up near the hide, or take it to the keeper with any other information like: 'I saw a stoat fifty yards down the hedge from my hide. I'm sorry I couldn't get a shot at it.' Offer pigeons to anyone who likes them, and in general act as you would if it were your own property.

Some of you who read this may feel hurt and think, 'Of

course, we do these things.' My friends, I make no apologies. I have said before, that it is the tiny minority who abuse and so lose the great majority their chances. You cannot be too careful, and that applies particularly to members of wood pigeon or other shooting clubs. On your own, a mistake costs you your shooting and it is doubtful if the door will be opened to anyone else. But a mistake by a club member probably affects all members.

Reconnaissance

If you plonked me down in any part wooded and part arable district of the United Kingom, with a car, a one-inch map of the area and a good pair of binoculars, for preference at about 2 pm, I could guarantee to say whether there were any pigeons operating in that area, and in due course to find the actual field they were feeding in. After a further look at this field I could tell you where to put the hide. This is no boast, it is a statement of fact and I make it simply because reconnaissance is the first vital step in successful decoying. I have already said that it helps your case considerably if, when asking the farmer for permission, you can start off by saying, 'You have a lot of pigeons on your one-year ley by that old black barn.'

How do you set about finding them?

Pigeons are gregarious feeders, that is to say they enjoy eating together, and what is more they like using the same restaurant while food and service are good. This charming though foolish habit is the cause of their downfall and makes decoying possible. What is more, they will come back after they have been shot at, and don't let anyone tell you differently! I know the cry, 'We had one shot and the —— never came back!' I don't pretend to make hard and fast rules about pigeons. Yesterday we started at

11 am in a field where the evening before I had seen about 400 birds on the clover, at about 5 pm. By 3 pm we had exactly 10 pigeons between us and there were some hard words from my companion who had been told he was in for a battle. Then they decided to come and by 6 pm when we packed up, the score was 210. We stuck it out and were right to do so. It is pretty certain that if they are really feeding on X field they will in due course come back to X field and not take long about it. And as this habit of feeding together on a chosen field is the basis of all pigeon decoying, you have simply got to believe in it, as I do. I too have had disasters (usually with someone who I hoped would have a good shoot). After careful reconnaissance of the field, with plenty of birds about, I have prepared the hide, set out the decoys and then waited, mouthing platitudes, and waited — until the bitter realization has hit me that they are not coming after all, and where on earth can I go to give him a shot or two!

And I have started off with a good shoot only to have it inexplicably peter out. But those days are very few, thank Heavens, and I say with confidence that if you go out 100 times, and see birds well and truly stuck into a field, on 95 of these occasions they will return and keep on doing so. I expect the reason for these lapses is either that they have finished the feed, found something more attractive, or moved on as a flock. But 5 per cent is not a bad proportion of failure, and you must really rely on their natural habits.

All this remains true in 1969, despite the stories one reads in the sporting press about pigeons not coming back. One still has disasters but not more often than before and faith in what your eyes have told you must still be the guiding principle.

In winter, pigeons set off to feed from their dormitories at dawn. Only the cock pheasant and the crow beat them to it. Thereafter, in winter and early spring, they stay around the field, or flight to it from another field, or a line of trees which they use as a rest or preening place. So hungry are they that they feed virtually all day, the green stuff being very rapidly digested. And as the weather gets harder this habit becomes all too obvious, as the tops of any kale will show. They act more or less in this way in early spring, though as the days grow longer, they are not quite so pushed and take things a little easier. Beech or other buds may keep them busy in the morning and they may not flight out to feed until midday.

After the middle of April pigeons definitely stay about the woods, and are very difficult to see because they are not sitting on the tops of the trees as they do in winter, before flighting out to feed. They are well down or even on the ground, making reconnaissance more difficult and patience rewarding. You simply have to watch until they give some clue as to what they intend to do and it may well be after midday before you get the answer. This continues until young kale or rape starts growing when they may well have an early morning feed and then start operations mid-morning. They will also feed on later and the new time should be borne in mind. I always used to say that 5 o'clock was a good time to pack up but of course this now means 6 o'clock.

In the summer months, when they have paired off, pigeons mostly fly to feed from the nest area. The days are longer and corn digests much slower than clover. It is difficult to state categorically that there are definite feeding times in summer. Perhaps one can say that they feed in the very early morning, and then there is a lull until about 1 pm when they start again, continuing until 7 pm or later when necessary. But you can find some pigeons feeding at all times of the day: it is this constant movement, if there are a lot of them, which makes their chosen field easy to find. This rather depends on the volume of what I call 'background', or, if you like, pigeon air bases. In areas where there are fewer pigeons in summer, there may be less well defined lines of flight from the nesting areas to a given field.

Whatever the time of year, pigeons use the same well-known flight lines if they can. These are usually noticeable features on the ground, such as strips, a ridge, a beech clump, a single tree, or a gap in a line of trees. You can usually see them as well as the pigeons can, if you know what you are looking for, which is the secret of all observation.

If you want to shoot pigeons in July or August you should look first for a likely background or nesting home. A one-inch map or your binoculars may well give you the answer, as you now know that small woods or blocks of forestry, strips or thick hedges are all potential nesting places. Then think of the crop they are most likely to be on at that date, probably autumn-sown wheat and badly laid at that. You, a novice in the gentle art of pigeon shooting, are out with me trying to find somewhere to shoot on ground new to both of us:

COATS: That looks a likely bit of background. Have a look with your binoculars and see if you can see any pigeons flying out from it. If you do, follow them along.
NOVICE: I see one, blast, I've lost sight of it.
COATS: Try again.

NOVICE: There's another, going in much the same direction. Now he's vanished too.

COATS: We'll move the car another 100 yards down the road to that gate; you may see better from there. Now have another look.

NOVICE: There's one going back to that fir strip. He went into a tree.

COATS: Probably going home. Look the other side of where you saw the first two disappear. Where exactly did they vanish?

NOVICE: That little square wood.

COATS: What's that crop on the other side? It's standing corn, but I can't see if it's wheat. See if you can spot a bird coming from the other direction. This game is rather like plotting with two or three compass bearings. X marks the spot where they·coincide!

NOVICE: Can't tell, I'm afraid. Oh, there are several pigeon in the air above the little wood. Now they've gone down again, right at the edge. Let's go!

COATS: No you don't. Keep watching. Any more traffic near that wood?

NOVICE (*impatiently*): Yes, there is movement from two directions.

COATS: Worth a closer look, anyway. That track should lead us pretty close. Take your time over this reconnaissance, it is never wasted.

The chances are that the novice will find the wheat (it might be barley) well laid next to the wood and may get a surprise as he walks along the headland. You can never tell how many pigeons are feeding on X field, particularly when the leaf is on the tree, until you go and put them up.

And even this can be deceptive as there are bound to be more on the nest which will come in due course.

Perhaps the best example of the art of spotting was at Woburn Park, where I used to shoot a lot of pigeons. The Park was a virtual sanctuary, surrounded by a wall and public roads which made observation by car simple. There were plenty of woods outside the Park, but the six lines from the Park were quite easy to see. On the first day, you simply stopped the car on the road near Line One, and got out with your binoculars handy and waited. In due course a pigeon appeared, winging out with that purposeful flight which characterizes the hungry bird who knows where he is going. You followed him until you lost him, then waited for a few more to go out. By taking the car along one of the numerous side tracks to 'the vanishing point', one more look usually supplied the answer, which was often in the 200 bracket.

In the winter, unless you are up at dawn, it is not much use looking at the woods or background. Pigeons are already on the feed. So put your binoculars on the likely places, one-year leys and permanent pasture, and in particular on any solitary trees or small clumps. They will be bare of leaves, so you should easily see any sentries or resting birds. My brother calls these trees 'sitty trees', and they are a very useful means of finding feeding pigeons, though they need not necessarily be next to the actual feeding field. By watching them, you will soon spot some bird fly off to join his pals, giving the game away. In some areas, it is quite simple to spot the birds on the ground, particularly on clover, and if there is snow it will be all too easy to find the poor things. Just look for the kale fields, they'll be there.

Needless to say, this is the hard, but also the most

rewarding way of locating pigeons. A little gossip in the pub, perhaps, quite apart from the farmer actually contacting you with information, is just as good and far less trouble! But I like to see for myself what goes on and then I have only myself to blame if something goes wrong. In the past, before I got rather cynical about the numbers people told me were on their fields, I used to get frightfully excited and think I was in for a big day. But now I don't believe anything until I see it. I have found that this leads to less disappointment.

I cannot sufficiently stress how very important are these two types of reconnaissance, first to find the real restaurant field, and then as in the next chapter, the correct place to put the hide. Almost everyone I take out wants to get cracking right away. This is understandable, but the old Army Manual precept that 'time spent on reconnaissance is never wasted' is dead right. But it is very difficult to tell that to the young!

HIDES AND HIDE SITING

Siting

Once you have established the exact field in which they are feeding, the second essential to successful decoying is the correct siting of the hide. Friends who have been out with me remark that I think like a pigeon — no one has yet said that I resemble one, but that no doubt will come. All this is not so foolish as it sounds, for thinking like a pigeon means producing a natural picture which the bird expects to see when flying into his chosen field to feed; this is my definition of decoying. It applies all the year round, whether the birds are eating young kale, wheat or clover in Hampshire, old potatoes in Moray, beech-mast in Kent or acorns in Sussex. You can even produce this picture outside your favourite roosting wood, or on a line of flight and prove that *Columba palumbus* is indeed greedy and gregarious in that he cannot bear to see Tom, Dick and Auntie Sue apparently eating their heads off (even on a most unlikely looking field) without joining them for a nightcap. I am afraid you will read of this 'picture' *ad nauseam* but I promise you that faith in the basic theory that pigeons will return to their chosen field and the proper build-up of a picture to welcome them are the two most important things in pigeon decoying. Everything else follows on.

If the pigeon is expecting to see a perfectly natural

picture, then this must be where he is expecting to see it. For one reason or another — the line of flight, the direction of their home or background from the field, or the placing of good 'sitty trees' — pigeons seem to favour an area or one side or end of a given field. So you must site your hide in that area under what I call the main *pigeon traffic*.

Thus it follows that the *geographical position of the hide is far more important than the direction of the wind*. I cannot emphasize this enough. It is frightfully important. Many people go wrong here and think that they have to site their hide so that the wind is behind them. Figure 1 shows

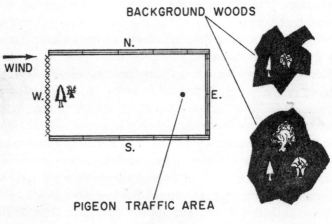

Figure 1

a 15-acre field which is rather long and narrow. The temptation is to make a bee-line for the west end, where there is a nice easy hedge with elder in it, very suitable for hide making, as well as some rather attractive looking 'sitty trees'. You can no doubt make a lovely picture at the west end, dead right for the wind too. But if the pigeon traffic is coming from the east, where all the background woods are, you may not do so well. So do not rush in or disturb the feeding birds. Watch the field and note where the birds are pitching. Check the line of flight in and out of the field and the general'pigeon movement. Better to take some trouble, even if it involves carrying nets or hide-making materials some distance, and be right first time, than have to move later on when your boob is all too obvious! One makes mistakes. I still do. But never adopt the 'I can't be bothered to move' attitude. Your bag will often be much heavier for a little trouble taken, and who knows, you might otherwise miss a red-letter day! Even thirty yards can make a difference, particularly on a line of flight. In theory you ought to be able to force pigeons to come to you by means of the decoys. And you may well do so under certain conditions, which I explain later under Advanced Decoying. However, first things first, and in pigeon shooting, as in everything else, Theory does not always work! So not only must you spend time on reconnaissance in an area to find the feeding field; time spent watching that field is never wasted, and may make or mar your day.

One further point, which should perhaps come under Advanced Decoying, but it is as well to at least consider it. I now try to think what the pigeons will do, in particular where they will come back from, once you have started firing. It is probably unneccessary in most cases, certainly with a bale hide, but I prefer more and more to try to push them up-wind of me, so that they can come back in their own sweet time. To achieve this, the area your shot will clear, and their subsequent probable return flight, can affect the site choice of the hide.

Types of Hide

So as soon as you have sited the hide to fit the pigeon traffic, then you must decide on the type of hide most suitable for that spot. Hides fall into three categories:

(a) Natural hides, made out of existing bushes or vegetation, usually with the aid of a hedgeknife or bill-hook. By far the best natural hide is made from the elder bush, which cuts and breaks easily, and can soon be shaped like a grouse butt, with about 180° field of fire and suitable peep-holes and background. Even in winter, by pressing down the bare stems on top of one another, you can build a fine hide in a matter of minutes. Elder also supplies suitable 4 in to 6 in sticks for sticking under the throats of the slain when putting them out as decoys, and also longer ones for use on posts or laid corn.

Branches can be cut, carried and stuck in the ground and tied together, though you always need rather more material than you would think and have to watch the background to this hide. These branch hides work satis-factorily in the middle of a field. It is always best to bend your handiwork to your satisfaction from inside the hide. It doesn't matter in the least whether the leaves are back to front. I don't think pigeons are that choosy.

A ditch can be a first-class hide when used like a slit trench. In Norfolk we used to 'dig in' in the soft loam of the dykes, and make a palatial hide with seat and shelves for all equipment, in about ten minutes. A plank to set across the dyke completed it.

A retracted hide can be made, for instance, in a holly bush. The main points about this hide are that it is always built some way into a strip or hedge, has a smaller field of fire and thicker cover all round. All these things add up

This hide does not work too well when put clean in the open, though if you have sufficient decoys to start with it may do so. I have used these nets in a slight hollow which provided a minimum of background. But even with the slender background of a wire fence, the net hide is a great success and I use it more and more. Other excellent sites for it are against a tree, or under the branches of a tree. In fact, anywhere where there is a little background and it would take you a long time to cart material. It takes three minutes to erect and you can carry three nets and five stakes quite easily with all your other kit. At least I can, my kit being simple. Those who need a pantechnicon to move their pigeon-shooting equipment around may have some difficulty. Canes instead of stakes are lighter, but do not make such a steady structure, are sometimes difficult to get into the ground and do not hold the net so firmly. You have to sit in a net hide, and sit still too. And it is better to shoot sitting down, for reasons which you will learn later on.

You stamp the pointed stakes into the ground with the 'kicker-in' provided, then drape the nets over the V-shaped uprights, leaving a curtain entrance with the last net. Then get inside, sit down and push the net about until you can see the decoys through the net and have a lower place to fire over, which will probably cover the killing ground. Try and make the back part higher than the front to give you more background. If you are thinking of having a set of stakes made, I believe it would be better to have two of them made 6 ft tall for the back and the remainder the usual 5 ft 6 in. I get extra height, when next to a barbed wire fence, by fixing the stakes through the wire. It was a long time ago, but I think the whole outfit, three nets and five stakes, cost me about £4. Nets can, of course, be used together with branches or other material, and I frequently use one net only and two stakes to cover a gap or cut-out bit of a hedge where there is still some background. All in all, nets have become an essential part of my pigeon-shooting equipment.

A 12 feet long by 5 feet high roll of wire netting with straw, hessian or bits of sacking tied on as camouflage is also quite good, though inclined to be cumbersome. This has canes threaded through it at intervals, and these are stuck in the ground, if the ground is willing!

Someone once showed me a very good light hide made of green raffia. You can make a hide of almost anything so long as it has some sort of background and you abide by the two vital rules of hide discipline: sitting still and looking *through* the cover. It is always wise to carry a portable hide of some sort in your vehicle.

(c) The bale hide. This is in a special class of its own, and not only because you have to get the farmer or one of his men to take it out for you. And let me say straight away that it is an old wives' tale that you have to put out a bale, or indeed any hide, for some days in advance to get pigeons used to it. I have frequently driven the tractor myself, dumped the bales, taken the tractor back, built the hide and shot 200. I am mad about bale hides, as you will no doubt find out. The drill with a bale hide is to ask your farmer to have fifteen or sixteen sound bales (thirteen is the minimum) loaded on a trailer at a convenient time. And by 'sound' I don't mean the sort that burst as soon as you touch them. Having previously reconnoitred the field and decided where to put the bales — which means right under the pigeon traffic — you return to the farm and drive your car as near to the field as you can get it, followed by the tractor and trailer. You then park the car, embark on top of the bales and ask the tractor man to drive into the field, directing him to the chosen spot. If you ask the farmer to have the bales put out for you, it is 7–4 on that they will be put at the end of the field farthest from the pigeon traffic. So, if your time is not convenient for the farmer, then stick a large bushy-topped tree in the field to mark the spot where you want the bales dumped. Then ask him please to tell the tractor driver that you have done so. I rather labour this point as it is unbelievable how often I have arrived at a field, having carefully planted a vast branch in the spot where I wanted the bales put, only to find them 100 yards away. And the explanation is always exactly what you would expect it to be!

Having unloaded the bales, you make the hide in a square, three bales up. This uses twelve. The thirteenth is a seat and number fourteen goes behind your seat as a fourth tier, as background, so that birds do not see you so easily if you get up to shoot. Any others are used for windbreaks, shade or blocking the entrance. A spare bale is always useful in case you have a casualty, though a broken bale is very useful for filling in odd cracks and putting bits across the 'joins' so that you can look under them. In any case, fluff out the straw where the bales join and look through this rather than over the top. I usually make the entrance on the side where I least expect pigeons to come, and simply put the bales at such an angle that I can squeeze through. But in winter your entrance must be down-wind and the up-wind side well sealed, lest you freeze. The draught in a badly made bale hide has to be felt to be believed. The top four bales can be placed on their sides, which gives another 2 inches height. This rather depends on who is to occupy the hide, and I have a lady shooting friend who is on the small side and doesn't need the top bale at all. Bale hides have to be sited correctly from the word 'go'. You try and move thirteen sodden bales even 50 yards. It isn't on. But these hides seem to act like a magnet to pigeons, and after a day or so you will find that they use them as perching places and you can put a decoy on top quite happily. I did this once, and caught a pigeon which landed, I think with evil intent, right on top of the decoy.

You can also use six bales the hard way by sitting on the ground with your back to two of them, one on top of the other. This provides your background. The others are arranged like a coffin with the last bale crosswise so that you have some cover when you sit up to shoot. Needless to say you have to sit rather still until you do shoot, but this hide can be quite fun, although it is not recommended for the aged. And the angle of fire is very restricted, unless you want to practise for the Twist.

Whatever hide you make, for goodness sake *sit* in it. Your angle of vision is far better: just try it and see. And you are far less obvious from the air — the angle from which the pigeon is looking. And you can look comfortably through the cover, net or branches or straw and not over the top. To make this easier, I usually site at least three peep-holes left, front and right. The background of any hide set out in the open is not always what you would like it to be, and therefore sitting down helps. Leave a reasonable entrance in any hide, as you will continually be going out to put out more decoys and tidy up.

Having decided on the best type of hide (you may have little choice), you will then get cracking. But before you start to make your hide, walk the pigeons off the field and, if they settle in nearby trees or a hedge, get them out of that too, right away from the field. Under 'Advanced Decoying' you will see that I sometimes advocate walking them up-wind, but for the moment content yourself with getting them away back to their background, if possible, so that they can return in their own good time. But *never*, *never* fire at them until you have your hide built and your decoys out. By doing this, which may seem a waste of time, you are simply ensuring that your first shot will not scare a lot of birds at once. Pigeons are probably quite used to being disturbed by farm vehicles, so they do not mind you walking them off at all. By the time they come back, you will have that nice little picture ready to receive them.

If I am making a hide in a hedge, I cut myself into it with my hedgeknife, make a rough emplacement, put the decoys out and start shooting. I finish the hide to my liking later on. So once you have decided on the site, get shooting as quickly as you can. The sooner you shoot, the sooner you will find out the pigeon reaction to the shot and whether you have made your hide in the right spot. So there is no point in making a magnificent hide in a hedge, only to find that you have to move. With other hides, which you have to carry, it is a bit different. They probably have to be put up properly or they will fall down. At least, mine do. So here again the bale hide wins as it takes three minutes to erect once the bales are on the site and then you put out the decoys and are in action. Nets are my second choice, if you can't get bales, and the same thing applies to them. As both are likely to be in the open where pigeons can really see the decoys, unless you are way out in your reading of the pigeon traffic, you are far less likely to have to move.

April 1969: no comment, really, but I think you have to sit and learn to shoot sitting down in a net. But if you can't do this then you must jolly well let pigeons get below the sky-line of your net before getting up. But you have to be pretty quick on the draw, particularly on the second shot and the game of letting one bird sit, taking number two as he comes in, and leaving the sitter for your second barrel, may pay off.

I still think it sensible and wise to use the choke barrel on your first bird, very often the second will actually be closer.

It might be better to use two 6 ft 6 in stakes at the rear of your hide to provide better background as you get up and if the sides of the net are high enough to conceal you and you move with the pigeon behind them, then the actual front of the net can well be low enough to shoot over.

Don't forget to take sticks to put under their throats with you to either bale or net hides, where there are none available to hand.

Equipment

At this point, I might as well tell you the equipment I use. When discussing this book, chapter titles and so forth with my publisher, I was asked: 'I suppose you will have a chapter on equipment?' Well, I won't and can't. It would be a very short chapter indeed! Pigeon decoying is a simple business really, based on a very few vital principles. So your kit is simple too, and its only function is to convert these principles into fact, in action.

You need a fairly heavy billhook with a blade which is man enough for a thickish branch. If you want to carry a pair of secateurs, to clip off annoying bits in the hide, or that bramble which curls itself so lovingly round your seat, do so by all means.

You need a few bits of string or baling twine to tie up odd ends of branches which persist in falling in the wrong place; and rather more string if you are going to build a branch hide in the middle of a field.

I like a tin to sit on. An empty 4/5-gallon oil-drum of a size which fits your particular anatomy comfortably. The sack in which you carry your billhook and your dead pigeon decoys (another sack for the dog to sit on is a good idea), when folded, normally covers the space below that sharp rim of the tin which can become most uncomfortable. I bang the rim on mine flat with a hammer. This allows me to swivel more easily. If I can drive the van right up to the hide, I use a nice fat cushion on the tin! Liquid aids to happy pigeon shooting, both for yourself and the dog, are always welcome, and that's about the lot.

I shoot sitting down a lot. I have taught myself to do this because there are any number of advantages. Some of these cover the actual sitting in the hide, from the movement and background angles. But the actual shooting advantages are that birds show up better against the skyline because you are lower. There is less noise, part of the concussion being absorbed by the hide. In such hides as the nets, I fit my peep-holes and the arrangement of the net to cover the killing ground space and the decoys. I will explain this under Setting Out Decoys and Hide Discipline. Also, don't forget, I shoot a lot and standing day after day can be very tiring. But why, people ask me, a tin, why no shooting stick? The answer is, because I can swivel my posterior on a tin, to almost any angle, whereas I would (and so would you) fall off a shooting stick, and any other *chaise de chasse* for that matter, if it had not got a firm base. No apologies for harping on this sitting-down business, for it makes a lot of difference. I have a friend who has had his tin made with a compartment which holds his sandwiches, beer, etc. This is very advanced, but not a bad idea at that! I tie some baling twine through the handle of the tin and knot it so that the top of the sack can be threaded through, and tin and sack slung comfortably on my back.

If you know that the cover in which you are going to set up your decoys is rather high, Figure 3 shows a useful

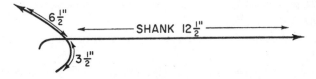

Figure 3

gadget invented by Charles Coles of the Kynoch Game Advisory Service. No doubt your local blacksmith can make one up for you, but don't sit on it!

Your gun is without a doubt best carried in a slip which has a sling attached. Thus your hands are free, unless you use stuffed decoys (as I do) which are averse to being chucked into a sack and are best carried carefully in a fruit basket or carton with a handle of sorts. I am very fond of baling twine which is most useful stuff. A year's supply can usually be 'won' without much fuss from any farm where stock has been winter fed.

How many cartridges should you take? It depends on what sort of a shoot you expect to have. I have a vast bag which takes 250, but if yours is on the small side, you can always put some more boxes at the bottom of the sack. People often say: 'It is so nice to go out with Archie, he puts you in a hide with a 250 box and says: "That should do you." ' But of course this is really because it is an awful bore to hear a cannonade from some place, wonder whether your friend is running out and have to stop shooting and motor over to see, especially if you are doing quite well yourself! Anyway, take more with you than you think you will need, and have some spare in the car. They don't go bad, or run away, unless you have a few friends like I have!

Personally I don't think you can beat a double-barrelled 12-bore, with improved cylinder in the right barrel for simple decoying shots, and half-choke in the left, for going-away second shots, and long shots. And the novice, whom you have met, will tell you in the chapter on Hide Discipline, to use your choke first if you are only going to get one chance. I use a side-by-side. I don't like the balance of an under-and-over for decoying. As for pump guns . . .! But no doubt I am biased. On the other hand, I am quite willing to back my preference if any under-and-over or pump addicts feel insulted.

I use no. 6 shot, Eley, Grand Prix, I always have done, I always will and I don't think there is a better cartridge made for pigeon shooting, or indeed for any other purpose. It is a British cartridge made with British materials by ici who know, and have known for years, what they are about. You can buy cheaper cartridges, some of them with foreign materials, and as far as I am concerned, you are welcome. My friends at the Kynoch Game Advisory Service at Fordingbridge have done much to further the cause of game and indeed pigeon shooting. It is without doubt due a great deal to their efforts that shooting in this country is now within the reach of far more people than it used to be. It does seem to me a little hard for people who have benefited from their efforts to buy cartridges elsewhere, quite apart from the quality question.

I always swore by size 6 shot. But much water has passed under the cartridge-making bridge since I wrote the above. Basically it is still quite true, but I now use almost exclusively 7's, all waterproof. I might use 6's for flighting or roosting, or wherever I think the pigeon might need a little extra stopping. But IMI have got a new crimp and a new wad and this definitely produces a tighter pattern with the 7's (at least on my bit of old newspaper). So for normal decoying these 7's now do a very good job on *Columbus palumbus* and those devilishly tough stock doves and at the same time I am not getting many 'walkers' and, you can put out decoys a good 35 yards away from the hide which makes that old picture just that much more broad and attractive.

As for game-shooting, I would think these 7's were now almost a 'must'! — but to judge from the incredible correspondence one still reads in the sporting press about choke pattern etc., some people still prefer 4's. However I suppose Editors have to eat!

SETTING OUT DECOYS

The 'Picture'

It has taken us rather a long time (a good deal longer than it does me!) to reach the stage where we must study the fascinating game of setting out decoys and making that natural picture which is so important. I am lucky in the winter months, as I can always keep a dozen or so dead pigeons back from the previous day's shoot. They keep quite well in winter, so there is no loss. In summer it is another story, and I cannot afford to lose that many pigeons through blowflies. So I use eight stuffed dead pigeons as decoys. These are without doubt the best decoy, other than a dead bird, which indeed they are to a certain extent. They can be placed anywhere and do not need propping up. But on laid corn, or a post, they look very lifelike. If the wind is strong they are liable to topple off, but a rubber band of suitable colour usually solves this problem. But let me again remind you that stuffed decoys require careful handling and must not be carried in a sack. Also, they do not like getting wet and it is better to take them in if it starts to rain, though I have an ancient set which look very ropey indeed, so I use them in wet weather and they still seem to work perfectly well. Unfortunately my source of supply has dried up. Alas, I am hopeless at 'do-it-yourself', but I believe that a little expertise in the use of formalin will do the trick. You peel the skin and feathers carefully from the breast and cut-off all the meat. Then eviscerate the pigeon, stuff all crevices with cotton wool soaked in formalin, putting back the peeled skin and either sew or more simply use a rubber band to keep it in place. Taking a leaf out of the hippie's book, use a syringe and give a succession of liberal 'shots' to the rest of the pigeon. A bit of wire cunningly placed will keep the head in a lifelike position. But once again, treat them kindly.

Another way to foil the blowflies is to bake pigeons in the oven, (not too high or they will 'brew up') and you will find that these last quite a time and you then chuck them away when their charm as companions has palled, and start all over again.

There are many artificial pigeons, wobblers and the like, on the market. They are quite good to start with, but I have never found one that did not shine in the sun, and I always replace them with dead birds as soon as I can get enough. There can be no doubt, despite all the advertising which almost leads you to believe that artificial decoys are better than the real thing, that dead birds are best and stuffed birds come a close second.

You set the dead birds out with a 4–6 inch stick stuck under or into the chin. You put all decoys, real or otherwise, about two to three yards apart. Not less. Now study a flock of birds feeding undisturbed. They do not all face the wind when they are feeding, and new arrivals often fly over their pals to the front of the line, jumping the queue if you like. The general tendency is certainly into the wind, but nevertheless, do not set your decoys out like a squad of guardsmen. The idea is to have a nice broad back or two covering any angle of approach, and this applies particularly if you are near a tall tree or hedge over which they may come. Thus they think that 'Old

Charlie' has just dropped off the tree to feed. It is an old wives' tale that cutting the eyelids off pigeons when setting them out will bring their pals down. And it is not necessary to have all your decoy's heads up in the air on sticks. Just lay some of them on the ground, or prop them up slightly on a bit of clover or whatever the crop is. Again, look at an undisturbed flock. There are a few heads up, perhaps as sentries, but most of them are getting down to it, which is what they are there for. In this way you present that natural picture I keep on talking about.

This would all be easy if I had not thrown a slight spanner in the works by stating categorically that the geographical position of your hide under the pigeon traffic is more, much more, important than the wind's direction. But it is, and, as the wind can be very perverse, you have very often to site the decoys so that the pigeons can come into them using the wind as they will, passing the hide at a reasonable killing range. The sketches will, I hope, give you an idea of one of the more interesting technical problems of decoying. In all cases I leave a space through which, or into which, I hope birds will fly and give me the best, the easiest, chance. Don't for one minute think that I mean the best sporting chance. I am out to kill pigeons, that is my job. My second shot may often be much more difficult or sporting, but I want one bird on the ground every time! So I call this space the killing ground and I try to make it about 30 yards away from the hide, whatever the wind's direction. This range gives about the best pattern for no. 6 shot, from an improved cylinder barrel. The second shot may be a bit farther out, but presumably your gun, like mine, will have some sort of choke in the left barrel, which will cater for the extra range. Figures 4 to 7 inclusive illustrate

decoying when the hide is in a hedge, by a tree or anywhere with a background which limits the arc of fire to
approximately 180°.

Figure 4. The straightforward shoot with the wind in
the right direction, blowing from straight behind you.
Farthest decoys about 30 yards — remainder 20–25
yards. A broad front.

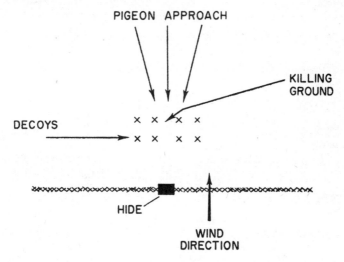

Figure 4

Figure 5. Wind dead against you. In this case set the
decoys much farther out, almost out of shot in extreme
cases. Most of them should face away from you, towards
the wind. Thus the pigeons will come between the hide
and the decoys to get into them against the wind. But
some will probably come in right over your head and be
too far out before you get a shot. Wait for these, don't
move, and the chances are that they will turn and come
round again. This wind situation usually means that the

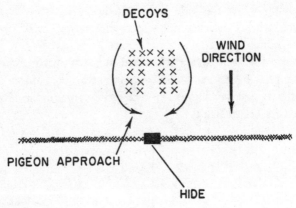

Figure 5

background to your hide must be better and higher than usual.

Figure 6. Crosswind from right of hide towards you. Farthest decoys about 30 yards out aslant the wind, on the windward side of the hide (in this case the right-hand side).

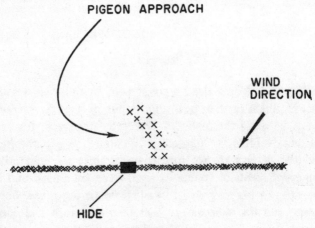

Figure 6

Thus birds can approach in front of and pass the hide to get to them. Nearest decoys may be 10 yards from the hide and I have ended up, with such winds, with a sort of semicircle. The reverse procedure for crosswinds from the left of the hide.

Figure 7. Wind from behind but across. Set the decoys, in this case to the left of the hide, some quite close, perhaps 10 yards. Thus birds cross your front to get to them.

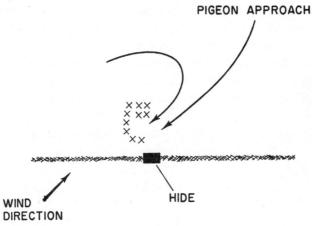

Figure 7

These are reasonable positions in which to set your decoys to start with. But they are not cast-iron and you will soon see what pigeons will do when they see your decoys and then you can alter their position accordingly to suit the killing ground. Don't take difficult shots; give them another chance to swing into the decoys — another bird may come giving you a better chance. You need a sort of 'third eye', which is really instinct, to tell you when and when not to take a bird, when an easier one is just behind it. But if you have to, use the choke barrel. After a little practice, you can tell by the way a pigeon is flying whether it is likely to come into the decoys, or whether it is wary and does not like the look of your picture. Any such doubtful starters immediately make me suspicious that something is wrong with the decoys — a bird on its back, for instance — and I check up.

Always build up. Set out more decoys and improve your picture. Use a lull to do this. You will often find that you will get many shots quite quickly and then there's a calm period when nothing happens. Why this is so, I do not know. It may be that a pigeon decides to flight to the field, others see it and follow on and so you get a little traffic. Anyway, you definitely get these lulls and you should use them to build up. *Decoying is compound interest*. The more you kill pigeons to build up that picture, the more they will come, and so it goes on. Shooting does not scare pigeons if they are set on coming into a field. I call this positioning of decoys, with its attendant killing ground 'channelling them in'. It really does work and is one of the major pleasures of decoying, being all your own work and very satisfactory to achieve.

A bale hide, or any hide set in the middle of a field, has great advantages over others. You have probably sited it plumb under the pigeon traffic, and they must be able to see the decoys very easily. And, in addition, you can cover every line of approach with decoys and shoot at any angle you want.

Figure 8 shows how I start, with decoys in the easy position, right for the wind. I always leave a pretty large space or killing ground between them, which I can fill in if necessary. Then I set out more decoys at all angles to the hide, so that birds coming from any direction have a chance

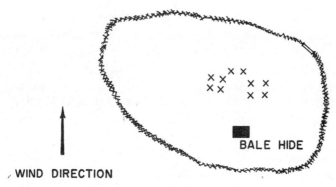

WIND DIRECTION

BALE HIDE

Figure 8

of seeing them. This does not mean that they will come into these other decoys, which might be right up-wind of you. Having seen them, they then spot the main body and will usually curl round and join them. But you can get a fine variety of shots, if you want them, because if it is pigeon etiquette to join feeding friends by flying up-wind, even at the last minute, there is apparently nothing to prevent a good beat-up on the way! For all these reasons it is not surprising that most of my really big scores have been made in bale hides, and I have no doubt that this will go on.

I am all in favour of setting decoys on a post in a fence, or on a bush, particularly where the cover in which your main body of 'deeks' is reposing is rather thick. This is the place for Charles Coles' gadget, as shown in Figure 3. If the crop is well up, incoming birds may well see the sentinel perchers more easily and so be attracted to those on the ground. But generally speaking, I do not use decoys in trees when shooting on the field where they are doing the damage. And for two reasons, the first being that they are coming to that field to feed and so the decoys on the ground (that old picture again) are surely enough. And secondly, I have said that my equipment was simple, and most lofting kits I have seen have been anything but that. I am not saying that it is wrong to loft a bird, but simply unnecessary. I have my own way of attracting passing pigeons' attention to my decoys, if I think they won't see them. I keep one or two dead birds in the hide, and lob or bowl them a few yards about hide-high towards the decoys. This game works better from a hide on a rise, or one without too much background which may prevent pigeons from seeing my thrower. It works very well from a hide under a single tree, as they presumably think that a bird has just flown off the tree to feed. I have even used it successfully from a bale hide. But sometimes it just doesn't work and seems to scare the daylights out of the birds, so you must try it out for yourself. At least it is quite simple, and you don't have to carry poles about as you do with lofters. Perhaps I am just idle and not skilled enough. Certainly other people have success with lofting birds, so maybe I am missing something. But I must say I have never thought, while decoying, 'if only I had a pigeon on that branch'.

Shooting roosting pigeons, with a decoy, or better still several, well up a tree is an entirely different matter and can be very successful. I still don't use them, as I feel that getting on the line is quite enough, and I can back myself to find the right spot. And the line can change and I hate to be tied to one particular place. The only lofted birds I have seen used with success were on permanent pulleys. They were windlassed up to branches of tall ash or other favourite 'sitty trees'. The chief drawback is that they may be wrong for the wind on the particular day. I once had a fine shoot on a platform, using lofted birds, but the wood was small, the wind was right, and I sometimes wonder whether they made all that difference.

April 1969: there is little to add. The correct and natural picture is all-important and always will be. It is often well worthwhile siting some decoys well to either flank or even behind you and indeed sometimes out of range, to allow birds that are by-passing you to see them. Remember, they will not come into these decoys but will obey the dictates of the wind and curl round to your main 'set-up'. For instance, in Figure 8 you could put decoys right behind the hide, if pigeons were crossing the wind, up-wind of the bales. They would then see the main body of decoys as marked in the sketch, and swing round, on either side of the hide into them.

But on the whole, every lecture I give stresses that this picture, its build up and the hide discipline and all that goes into it, is the real answer to the success of your day's shooting. And so for those who are not brilliant performers and have difficulty in setting this compound interest system going, it is probably wise to spend a little money on a goodly number of decoys to start the ball rolling.

Hide Discipline

Well coached by me, you, the novice whom we have met before, have successfully driven the birds off the field and are now comfortably settled in your hide. The decoys are out and the stage is set. If your reconnaissance has been right and they *are* feeding in that field and you *have* sited the hide in the correct place, there is nothing more you can do. The die is cast. You must just wait, and if they are keen at all, it won't be long before your first customer is with you. Incidentally, I shoot the first one quick. It is another fable that you should let the first one in unscathed. I tried this once, and he simply fed beside the decoys, though looking at them with a slightly hurt expression. He might have been there for hours, if another one hadn't come in. So I got fed up and plugged them both. It really doesn't make any difference, and very often I have hardly time to take the slip off the gun and sit down before there is a bird on the decoys. You do have to wait sometimes, and occasionally I have started the ball rolling by firing a shot, usually on large downland areas of clover which I knew I had to keep clear by the power of the shot. But I don't like doing it, and, on a single field of some definite crop, it may be a confession of failure, though not always. If I wait fifteen minutes under such circumstances without a taker, I am worried, and if I wait twenty-five minutes, there is something wrong and I may well fire a shot to see what happens.

Those who wait for hours have more patience than I; and I would not do so, without a good reason such as seeing them there the day before. I would know that the whole basis was wrong; either I had made a mistake and they were not feeding on that particular field, or it was one of those 5 per cent days when they just weren't going to play. I would then try elsewhere. I realize I am lucky looking after several areas each with completely different lots of pigeons. So I do not lack for fresh ground, though it may mean driving some miles.

Anyway, let us hope that all is well. But since I last saw you, writing this book has so exhausted me that I am but a shade. So you, poor novice, are going to have to suffer my invisible but audible spirit sitting in the hide with you. The idea is to teach you a little hide discipline. Like most discipline, it eventually makes life (and the shooting) easier for you, although you may think it is a bore to start with.

COATS' SPIRIT: Well, those decoys look fine to me, let's get in the hide.

NOVICE (*having taken his gun out of the slip and looked through the barrels in a very correct manner*): Shall I load my gun?

COATS (*very restrained*): It might be a good idea, but get yourself comfortable first.

The Novice sits down on the tin, wriggles a bit and looks hopefully towards the decoys.

COATS: While you are waiting, make certain your peep-holes are sited so that you can look through them, at the decoys, and not over the top of the hide.

NOVICE: I can see them fine now, but the tin seems a bit near the front of the hide; I don't think my gun will come up very quick.

COATS: OK, alter your position till you can either shoot sitting down, or stand up. But remember, if you stand up, you must do so and fire in one movement.

At that moment a pigeon comes in and settles amongst the decoys.

COATS (*whispers*): Go on, what are you waiting for?

NOVICE: Go on, what?

COATS: There's a pigeon on the decoys. Shoot the —— thing. On the ground if necessary.

NOVICE (*peering through the cover*): I can't see it.

COATS: Well, you altered your seat but not the peep-holes, so now they don't fit. Get up quickly and have a go as he flies off.

Novice does this but the bird is out of range before he fires.

COATS: Never mind, not quite quick enough. Look out, here comes one from the right. He is coming in, can you see him? Fire straight at him when he is in that space, the killing ground I told you about.

NOVICE (*as pigeon flies away before being shot at*): Oh blast, I forgot and looked over the top and I'm afraid he saw me. Shall I put my mask on?

COATS (*sotto voce*): Why do I do this? (*aloud*) No, masks are quite unnecessary if you sit still and look through the cover. But a hat or a cap with a good brim is essential.

NOVICE: There are three coming from the left, I think they are turning this way. Yes, they are; which shall I take?

COATS: The easiest, and let them come right in before you fire — wait — *now*.

Novice fires and scores with one barrel, missing with his left.

NOVICE: Blast, I should have got two.

COATS: Nonsense, be content with one to start with and let the Lord provide you with your second shot; you will soon get into it. Anyway, well done, any more about? — If not we'll go and stick that one up.

NOVICE: Can't see anything; let's go, I've got some sticks all ready.

At once a pigeon comes over the hedge, sees the decoys but leaves in a hurry when he catches the Novice in the act of leaving the hide.

NOVICE: Damn.

COATS: It can't be helped. You often get caught out. But you have got to use the lulls to build up that picture, and you will be caught out whatever you do. The one thing not to do is to run back to the hide. Just walk slowly back and he may still come on. Here's another. This one's all yours.

NOVICE (*after killing bird rather nicely with his second barrel*): How on earth did I miss him with my first? He was practically stationary above the decoys.

COATS: You may well ask; I expect you shot under him,

but let me assure you that I have seen some of the best game shots in the country miss sitters like that. Killing them is a knack you learn by practice. At least you didn't use the language the crack shots usually do!

NOVICE (*after killing and missing a few more birds*): I like shooting sitting down. The first shot is fine, but I am not too happy with the second. I wish I could get a right and left.

COATS: You will. You have a chance now, if those two come in. The drill is this; let the first one settle, or anyway come close, and take the second as he is coming in. Then get the first as he is going off. You'll have time. Here they come.

NOVICE: Good Heavens, I got them. It worked.

COATS: Thank you very much.

NOVICE: Can't they hear us talking?

COATS: They don't seem to worry about noise, certainly not shots. I think their eyes guide their actions far more than their ears, and yet I've seen them come into decoys when I was in the hide talking to someone who had just driven up in a Land Rover to see how I was getting on. Used to farm vehicles too, I expect. They can be remarkably foolish, you know.

NOVICE: I say, do you notice that some of them are coming almost over the hide, and they see us?

COATS: Yes, you're right, our background seems to have fallen down a bit. You'd better cut a decent branch, no, not that young beech, that elder five yards along will do. Now let's put it behind us like this. That's better, they won't see us now as long as you sit still. For Heaven's sake don't cut valuable timber for a hide or I'll get the sack.

NOVICE: How many have I got?

COATS: About 15, but you're learning. We had better put some to the right and so try to bring these so-and-so's in a bit nearer your hide. They seem to pass too far out. How's that?

NOVICE: Can one really channel them?

COATS: Yes, usually, if they obey the wind, but sometimes they seem to disobey the rules, rather like you!

NOVICE: How many dead pigeons do you set out as decoys?

COATS: That's a good question. I suppose the answer is almost always every bird I shoot until there is no doubt that any bird coming into the field within a reasonable area can see the decoys. It is rare to set out more than 60 or 70; then you simply pick up any others. But always set out fresh birds with a purpose; to improve your picture and eventually make it perfect so that every bird enters your killing ground.

NOVICE: I saw you pick up that bird lying on its back. Why?

COATS: I always try and keep the picture as it should be. Pigeons don't expect to see their chums on their backs or too many feathers about, although I don't think the latter make much odds. But always tidy up the decoys in the lulls at the same time as you set more out. By the way, the same thing applies to your hide when you leave. Take away all your sandwich paper and cartridge boxes too. You can leave the cases unless there are any stock, especially pigs, which might eat them. But don't destroy your hide; I use the same hides over and over again, very often a particular field comes back to the same crop in due rotation. Look out, there's a carrion crow coming. Keep absolutely still and don't move an inch until you fire.

Novice fires both barrels.

NOVICE: I hit him. I know I did.

COATS: Not hard enough, you horrible boy. That's just the sort of thing that gets me good marks with the keeper.
The crow suddenly towers and falls at the far end of the field.

COATS: My apologies, you got him after all; we'll pick him up afterwards and hang him up by that tunnel trap down the hedge. The keeper will see him there.

NOVICE: Why did he come so close?

COATS: Crows are suckers for pigeon decoys and often investigate. You often shoot other winged vermin which is using the hedge or strip your hide is in. It's probably their normal line of flight. I once had a sparrow hawk stoop and hit a dead pigeon so hard that it impaled itself on the stick on which the pigeon's head was stuck up. If you see anything else, like a stoat and can't get it, tell the keeper where you last saw it.

I shouldn't hold your gun at the ready all the time. I find it rather tiring. Put it against the hide. I always make a safe place to hold it if there isn't one. Just watch your decoy area and if you see movement, then take the gun up. But do it when the birds are below the level of the hide and can't see the movement.

NOVICE: Should I unload the gun when I leave the hide?

COATS: Yes, if you have a companion. When I am by myself I don't, though perhaps I ought to. Anyway, unload it, as you quite rightly did when you crossed the fence to pick up that wounded bird. Better safe than sorry at all times.

By now lunch has been eaten in the hide (proper pigeon shooters don't stop for lunch and thereby ruin the continuity of their shoot), and the afternoon is wearing on.

NOVICE: Why on earth do they keep coming? I've fired nearly 80 cartridges.

COATS: Heaven knows; all I know is that this is their custom and I rely on it for my job. They won't quit until about 5 pm, although the last half-hour may be slacker. Most of them will have found somewhere else by then. They'll tell you when they've had enough. It is rather like a tap being turned off. On the other hand, if they are really keen on a field, your last half-hour may be very productive, and they can get quite silly about it, throwing themselves at the decoys in a frantic endeavour to feed.

NOVICE: Two birds went into that oak about 200 yards away — I saw one of them fall — should I go and get it?

COATS: No, not yet. Leave all far-out birds until the end. If you get them now you'll waste good shooting time, and as sure as anything you'll send another one straight there and have to go out all over again. And, by the way, in the nesting season, you'll have to be jolly careful not to poke about in hedges for birds, or you'll put your great foot on a partridge nest. And you won't shoot pigeons here again and neither may I, which is more important. There is an exception to this rule about picking up at the end; if a bird towers about 150 yards or so beyond the decoys, as likely as not pigeons will go down to it, which is a bore. So you must go and get it.

NOVICE: Why do you tell me to clap them off when they sit out of range beyond the decoys?

COATS: This is another basic rule of hide discipline. *Never* allow a bird to sit in the field you are decoying other than on your decoys, even if it means firing a shot. They're much more likely to do this on a still day, or if your picture is not all it might be. They love flying about on windy days, and usually come into the decoys much better. You probably get more movement in the dead birds' feathers, and maybe they see this. They also come on a more direct line which is easier to channel.

There is a heavy shower but the Novice is still very much on the ball and watches the decoys as if they might take off.

COATS: You can relax, pigeons don't like flying in the rain, sensible creatures. Rain is equal to a lull, so use it accordingly. They will start again when the shower eases off.

NOVICE: Can I smoke, I mean, not just now, but at any time?

COATS: Why not? I don't think they mind, but don't brew up my hide like some others have done.

They are slacking off now, it's nearly 5 pm, which seems to be union hours in the pigeon world. But one more thing before we pack up: if I want to punch you on the nose, but know that I will only have one chance of doing so, obviously I hit you as hard as I can. So, if you have a long shot and realize you will have only one chance, always use the choke barrel. It pays off and I don't see why it shouldn't apply to game as well. Anyone who can really hit pigeons, decoying or in any other way, should have little trouble with game, however well shown. But I fear the reverse is not always the case, as is proved by the Elizabethan English I have heard echoing across the downs from time to time.

NOVICE: Well, thanks very much for the help, I enjoyed it, and it was nice to feel I had some part in it and had to do some work for my sport.

COATS: Yes, that is one of the charms of pigeon decoying.

Anyway, you did well for the first time, but don't think you will always fire 90 squibs off every time you go out.

This hide discipline does help to produce a workmanlike and efficient approach to pigeon-shooting. The various points I have mentioned may seem trivial, but taken as a whole they make some sense.

Since I wrote the above, I have met few people who have had much success with this 'throwing' act which I practise. It is true that sometimes it really scares pigeons, in which case stop or try a different angle. But sometimes it does work, and from a considerable distance. I now crack the wings of a dead pigeon, which gives more movement as I throw. I don't throw very high or very far and I may well have a few pigeons about 10 yards from the hide into which I throw the 'chucker'. But it works best if the hide is near a tree, maybe they think the bird is going down to join the boys. But it is the angle at which you throw which is really important. If you are in a hedgerow they are unlikely to see a bird thrown out against the background of your hedgerow. Wait until they practically disappear from sight, as they are by-passing you on either side and time your 'chuck' so that they will see it sideways just as they are about to cross the hedge. But try it, it can do no harm and you may be pleasantly surprised.

Finally, I think it is kinder to pick up plastic cartridges from your hide, especially if there is or will be stock in the field.

ADVANCED DECOYING

It is not difficult, once you know the basic principles of decoying, to find a field and be very successful. But there are times when nothing obvious presents itself, though there are plenty of birds about. On these occasions a little extra cunning, allied to local knowledge, will give you great fun and not a little satisfaction, because success will depend a good deal on your correct reading of the situation. And don't forget, though my principle is to kill pigeons where they are doing the damage, one bird killed in any way is one less to breed. It may be doing no harm at the moment, but don't miss a chance to 'do' it. It is unbelievable how many otherwise quite sensible people fail to see this.

Many of these methods involve trying to force birds down to decoys on a field on which they are not really feeding at all; and to present a picture which some of them will take as real, and to build up that picture, so that it becomes more attractive. Therefore the more decoys you start with the better — and the more accurate you are, then better still.

Pigeons on the Welsh Marches are not as sophisticated as our Hampshire and Berkshire birds. So I thought it was a piece of luck, some years ago, when one mild afternoon in late January, about 1.30 pm, I chanced to see a dozen birds sitting on a pasture outside a good roosting wood. There were a few more in the trees, and I thought, 'That's funny, I know they are not feeding here regularly, as I shot the only cock pheasant for miles here this morning and there was not a pigeon in sight.' 'Quists' flight at dawn to the hills on either side of the Wye, to the sorrow of the local sheep farmers, whose rape and clover suffer. Having some dead birds in the car (just in case), I decided to set them out where the pigeons were feeding, and wait for a couple of hours until the evening flight. I simply sat with my back to a tree, about 10 yards inside the wood. The usual west wind blew from me towards the decoys. (I wish it was 'usual' when I am fishing the river, a scream-ing north-easter usually being my lot!)

Nothing happened for about five minutes; the pigeons I had put up seemed to have vanished. Then one came over the wood, appeared to see the decoys, and sat in a nearby tree. A start, but as it fell (all right, I shot it sit-ting), it stuck in a branch, so I had to push it down. I noticed that under this tall ash tree and others near it, the ground was covered with droppings. Now although it was the leeward side of the wood, it seemed to me that only a very rugged pigeon would choose those trees to roost in. They were right on the edge of the wood. Draughty, to say the least. Several birds then started to come and some of them definitely saw the decoys and then came into the trees. A few actually pitched on the ground. All this was new to me and most heartening. I kept on putting birds out until there was an imposing array and there was no longer any doubt — it worked! These birds were all full of clover or rape, so that it was just pure greed and habit. I was getting so much shooting that there seemed no point in moving back into the wood as roosting time approached. My shots disturbed the far end of the wood and very often pigeons got up, flew around, saw the decoys,

1. The van is loaded with all the pigeon shooter's equipment: gun, cartridges, decoys, hide, billhook, oil drum to sit on — and a bottle of beer.

2. Reconnaissance. Time spent on this is never wasted.

3. Building the hide.
(*above*) A natural hide in the hedge of a wood, this should take about five minutes to construct.
(*below*) A fence or hedge like this is quite sufficient background for a net hide, note the steel rods used to support camouflage netting.

4. Building up the decoy picture.
(*above*) Setting up the initial picture.
(*below*) You can't have too many decoys.

5. These photographs show how a short stick is used to prop up the heads of the dead birds when setting up the picture.

6. Throwing a dead bird out from the hide can sometimes attract passers by.

7. Net hide in the open. A bird coming into the decoys is shot, and retrieved by Simba.

8. The evidence.

(*above*) A cropful of freshly-drilled barley, a pigeon can eat up to a thousand grains of barley in a day.

(*below*) A freshly-shot bird that has been feeding on clover, a pigeon will eat three to four ounces of clover at a 'sitting'.

and apparently thought all was well. Only for the last ten minutes did I move back into the woods. I stopped with enough light left to enable me to pick up the decoys.

I could not wait to try it on the Hampshire birds, half expecting that there would be some derisive pigeon laughter, and no takers. However, it does work — outside Norfolk 'stops' and those nice little Wiltshire 'round-woods'. One thing I did find out. It is better to choose fresh ground for this game, so that pigeons may stuff themselves naturally and so be able to come home early. If you have been harrying them all day, they obviously stay late feeding.

May I suggest to those who can only get off work at lunch-time on Saturday, that this idea may give them a couple of hours more shooting. Many people only think of roosting as an hour's shooting, as indeed it is normally, but this plan gives you a chance to get a few before the actual roosting starts. Watch those tall ash trees or single beech trees. They are often 'sitty trees' used before birds go farther in to roost. As the days grow longer and they have more time to feed, a few replete birds may come in early. And these will be unable to resist joining their pals for a nightcap. Though a small wood is best, as they are more likely to see the decoys, your shot disturbs a large area and they see your picture. Even decoys on a fallow field will bring in a few, though a ley is better. Start with as many as possible. I sometimes decoy elsewhere until about 1.30 pm, when there is often a lull, presumably because they are tired of being shot at and have gone to a quieter spot. Then I take the hint, pack up and move to the roosting wood, setting about 20 of my morning's bag out as a nice trap for the unwary. You have to work for this, to make pigeons come in to somewhere where they

D

are not normally used to feeding; I repeat, use all the decoys you can manage. A sack takes 50 comfortably; so hump 20 birds across that plough, shoot another 30 with their aid and you will have a nice load to carry back! Never mind the wind, the 'sitty trees' are the attraction, unless your observation tells you that there are other 'sitty trees' used in certain winds. If the wind is wrong, just set out the decoys at one of the angles explained in 'Setting out Decoys'.

Perhaps this is the place for a lofted bird or a permanent pulley, but I can assure you that it works without either. This game is great fun, being decoying in its purest form and can be extremely productive. Figure 9 shows the set-up.

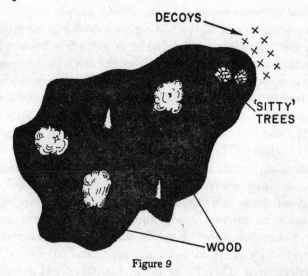

Figure 9

Some time ago I went to shoot pigeons on the Norfolk fens. Never having been there before, I was appalled when I arrived and saw only a few rather scraggy Scots pine strips, locally called 'stops'. Most of these were not more than 20 feet tall.

'Where do the pigeons live?' I wondered. But there they were, lots of them, mostly feeding on old potatoes, and though there were some 'background woods' some miles away, they roosted quite happily in the 'stops'.

It was here that I had some good 'dawn flights'. This can be fun for an hour or so, but there are a few points to remember. You must know the evening before not only that they are really feeding on X field, but also their approach line from the roost. You must have your decoys out and hide built before the first bird arrives. You will not have much time to go out and pick up as they come very quickly, and are hungry, and therefore not too particular about the look of things. Finally, it is no use staying there too long. They quickly tire of this game and go off for breakfast elsewhere. You must then find somewhere else, in the normal way, for the rest of the day.

I have to look after some downland farms which are indeed open spaces, comprising many hundreds of acres of clover, all of which is potential feeding ground, with very little cover. Nice warm bale hides in strategic positions and my wife doing a sort of cowboy act in our van are the only answers. Sometimes it pays to hang one or more bangers on the wire fences, to keep them on the move. Bangers can be quite useful, for instance when birds are feeding on two stubbles fairly close to each other, but yet too far apart to be covered by the noise of your shot.

I rely enormously upon what I call 'the power of the shot', to keep birds moving on the downs. Though there is such a large choice of feed, there are always one or two fields which they seem to prefer. And to show the gourmet side of their character, these are often the young first-year leys with the tender clover. So the awful question of where to site that lone bale hide in a sea of clover is often settled for you by their greedy habits. I start off with as many decoys as possible to give them every chance of seeing them. I sometimes take as many as 30 dead ones to start with. At least when they see them they are down in a flash, and, as usual, the more you shoot the better it is. But they must be kept on the move; and so must you, as it can be a very cold business.

Lines of flight play an important part in the pigeon's parochial life. As he prefers certain areas year after year, so does he use the same routes to his feeding grounds. You now know what these physical features are, and you also know that there are usually 'sitty trees', regularly used as a digestive club or watch-tower, somewhere near at hand. There may be a choice of several equally luscious clover leys in the area and sometimes it is difficult to tell which is the most favoured. So, provided pigeons are regularly using these trees, even if these are not situated on the feeding fields, and provided that your shot will keep the area fairly clear, it may pay you to build your hide by these trees, instead of taking a chance on one of the fields. My pastime of throwing out dead birds from the hide usually works well in this sort of shoot, but if nothing happens in the first few minutes, fire a shot. This should set the ball rolling and you can gradually build up a picture by keeping them on the move. This might apply to a situation where birds were feeding over the boundary, but would be happy to come on to the 'sitty trees' where you are lurking.

I have had several amusing shoots in north Hereford when staying with a friend of mine. His house stands well above the River Wye and 75 yards below the house is a strip of tall oak trees about 150 yards long, lying east-west. Below this the ground falls away very steeply to the railway and the river. There are large oak woods above and north-east and north-west of the strip, but over a quarter of a mile distant. On this particular day there was a strong west wind blowing.

A lot of pigeons were about, feeding on acorns, and there seemed to be a sort of circular movement from the north-west wood downward, and then back up-wind via the strip. Though the wind was strong, they were very high, by virtue of the lie of the ground, and I made several changes until I found a spot, a stand on an old uprooted stump, which gave me a few feet extra height. There I managed to get on terms. Having no decoys to start with, I had to kill some very high curling birds, like tall pheasants, before I could set some out. Even then, I could only set them out 100 yards down-wind of where I was standing. However, this brought a few much lower, and the score started to mount. It was then time for lunch, although I could hardly bear to leave this magnificent shoot. My conscience as a guest won, but only just.

Through the dining-room windows I had the agonizing spectacle of droves of birds streaming over my stand, but, most unusually for me, managed to resist second helpings and coffee, and dashed back again with more cartridges. By building up until I had about 40 decoys out I made them believe that the acorns here came straight from Fortnum's, and finished up with a respectable score. Poor Simba was very tired of fetching birds up the hill.

The point of this is that even with a large selection of acorn feeds about (or it might be beech-mast), the use of decoys will channel pigeons and bring them down. And

this, even if you are not right on top of the decoys. All
you want is the line of flight. It is the old story again —
present the right picture and the greedy woodies will fall
for it.

The same sort of thing can be done in a wide ride, a
clearing in a wood or outside a beech strip, that is if you
can get permission to shoot. Needless to say, this is not
always easy as most woods are potential pheasant stands.
In a game country, a large beech or acorn year may be
quite maddening, as you obviously can't disturb the
coverts.

Perhaps the best example of line of flight shooting I
remember was in Berkshire, in a very good (or should I
say bad) pigeon area. There was a wheat field, only slightly
'blown', and the pigeons were not particularly interested
in it. But it was on a line of flight from a block of forestry
to a favourite area of woods. Next to the wheat there was
a fallow field, and along the fence between the two stood
an old hut. There was also, in those days, a water trough
which was much favoured. I have used a convenient elder
bush beside the hut as a hide in the last few years, whenever the adjoining fields were suitably bare to set the
decoys on. There, time and again I have proved my
theory that you can make pigeons come down to decoys
if you set enough decoys out. This first time I started off
with three stuffed birds only. To begin with they took
no notice and I had to kill them on their line. But, as soon
as I had got a sufficient picture, some of the pigeons flighting back and forth simply came in as if it has been the
best feeding ground in the area instead of a patch of bare
earth. Sometimes I had to wait until the corn was cut
before using this hide. But it always worked, though
there were plenty of other stubbles. This sort of thing is

most satisfactory and is to me the epitome of pigeon shooting. It is to a great extent 'all your own work'.

Recently, two of us played much the same trick. We put net hides on the line of flight and decoys between us, well out on a late-planted mustard field, to lower them a little. We built the decoys up until the birds were coming in quite well, although they were full of grain and on their way home. This time it was a case of curiosity killing the pigeon.

This line of flight build-up is not to be confused with setting decoys out on any bare field next to the actual field they are feeding in. This latter method is simply another way of killing pigeons on the field they are damaging, and is most successful, particularly in summer. Say you wish to shoot a field of wheat which is not much 'blown', or perhaps 'blown' only in the middle where you can't get at it, or risk the wrath of the farmer if you do. If there is a ley, or better still, young kale or mustard next to the field, pigeons will almost certainly be accustomed to sitting on this bare field and then flighting in to feed. In dry weather a fallow will do equally well. Watch the line, make your hide on the edge of the wheat and set your decoys on the bare field. Put some on the dividing fence posts if there are any. The great point is that they can see your decoys perfectly. Given the choice, I far prefer to use this method than decoy a small patch of wheat where they might not see the decoys so well. If the crop is 'flat', it is another story and you should obviously make your picture on it. Needless to say, you have to keep them off the wheat by clapping, but your shots should keep them moving. When they see your build-up, it will seem the natural thing to do to join the party. A net hide is particularly suitable for this job.

In winter when dutifully putting pigeons off the field before shooting, it often pays to push them up-wind if there are suitable belts or 'sitty trees' where they can rest until they feel like a little refreshment. Even a fallow field will do, if you know they are using it as a resting place prior to flighting in to feed. The noise of your shot is muffled by the wind, and the ideal case (which I have seen happen once or twice) is that birds flying down-wind to feed see a pigeon fall, hear nothing, and think he has just landed amongst his pals! If the whole pack is downwind of you, your first shot may give you a fast first few minutes. On the other hand you may scare the daylights out of too many at a time, and it may take until the afternoon for them to drift back. In such cases it may be wise, when too many birds are on top of you, not to shoot at all. Let them go upwind and then come back of their own accord. Do not confuse this case of one particular field with that of the large area of clover already mentioned, where your only chance is to keep them moving and deny them the use of as large an area as the power of your shot will allow.

The place where the retracted hide comes into its own is the site on which you don't want to make too much noise. So, the last example given is a suitable occasion for its use.

Figure 10 shows a retracted hide in a thick double hedge. It is hoped that the decoys will either turn birds into the two 'sitty trees', which are both in range, or make them settle on the ground. The hide is constructed so that a shot can be taken only at these two chances.

A retracted or 'silent' hide does not need to be in a hedge. I recently had an amusing shoot on laid wheat outside Micheldever Forest, which is a good example of the

background of the beech. My shot was partly muffled, but still strong enough to put up at the other end of the field. But I was firing away from the forestry and so did not disturb incoming birds. Those who came in too low to be shot at, and pitched, were simply 'walked up' over the rim of the pit. As it was rather late, some of these birds had their crops partly full. Those who keep hens might note that the contents of any pigeon's crop, whether grain, clover or other green stuff, are always welcome as free chicken feed.

Last year, when on my rounds, I went to look at a certain autumn-sown wheatfield which, from its position on a good line of flight, I expected to be attacked, if it had 'blown' at all. When I got there I was horrified to see that the cattle must have got in and stayed in for some time, as it was badly trampled for a considerable area, in particular round a lone beech tree which I have long known as a good 'sitty tree'. There were some pigeons flying about, but I noticed that the few which got off the ground did so at the bottom end of the field near a hedge where the crop did not appear to have gone down much. Only 150 yards away, the beech tree looked most promising, so I made a net hide beneath it and set out the decoys. I could not understand why they would not come. A favoured tree, about two acres of feeding ground as flat as a pancake — all they wanted, you would think. Perhaps they were choosy about the many reminders of the cattle's presence. In the end, I had to move to the place where I'd seen them get up, a very small laid bit, where I eventually got 35. I later discovered that the cattle had been there only the day before, and presumably the pigeons had not found the newly knocked-down part, and anyway were happier on the bit they were used to. I went back four days later and killed 64 under the beech tree. They had found it. It is easy to be too clever and confuse what your eyes and the rules tell you with too much technical knowledge!

There is not much 'advanced' about decoying pigeons in snow. It is no good. They simply do not see the decoys even if you brush the snow off the roots or kale and place them on the top. Even artificially moving decoys or throwing seem to have no effect. I asked a renowned camouflage expert at Cambridge University why this was so, but he could offer no explanation. I think the simple answer is that the snow blinds them.

If they have little choice of feed, pigeons will keep returning to the field. The best way is for one or more guns to walk them off the field, back up their line of flight, and then line out behind a hedge. They will return like driven partridges (or anyway, rather poor driven partridges!). Those you shoot will be difficult to find and a dog will not long appreciate searching soaking wet kale with avalanches of snow cascading on top of him. Anyway, half of them won't be worth picking up. If there is no cover available, wear an old white sheet or milking overall and sit or stand quite still until you shoot. Personally, pigeon shooting in the snow is not my favourite pastime, though I hasten to add, in case one or two people I can think of read this, that it has to be done for the sake of the cattle or sheep feed. If the field is reasonably small, a bale hide is probably the best answer; at least it is warm. But don't forget to cover your bale seat with another bale before you leave, to keep it dry.

I have never made a big bag on a snow-covered kale field, and I am not sure that I want to. It is about the only time I feel sorry for the poor things. Sitting hunched and miserable on the kale, their digestive systems working overtime, they seem to know the end is not far away and the carcases lying in the hedgerows, so light that you wonder how they have survived so long, are a travesty of those healthy birds, revelling in their flying power, who came lilting into the clover, maybe only a week ago, so quickly does the cold's grip affect them. Selous loved elephants, though he probably killed more of them than any man; so perhaps I can be forgiven for being rather fond of, and indeed admiring, pigeons, despite their many sins. I hate seeing them in this pitiable condition.

Another way of making a good bag is to use the pigeons' habit of going to some shady trees or woods for a rest between meals. There may be a water trough or pond nearby, or they may roost there later on. Anyway, they must be very fond of it and use it a lot, and only local knowledge and observation will tell you the few woods which are their favourites.

I know of such a wood, mixed beech and pine, which stands rather alone surrounded by a large acreage of arable land. I use this wood for two purposes. In the winter, it is a first-class roosting wood with or without decoys to start with. But come October, when there are usually a lot of pigeons at the stubbles, they use this wood to rest in all day long and then roost there in the evening. With a good wind, two guns can set out decoys to channel them and have a really good shoot. You either stand in hides at the edge of the wood or, leaving your decoys, go farther back on a ridge where there are several gaps. You can start at 10 am and go on till 4.30 pm. The pigeons then tell you that it is time to pack up and you won't get many coming in to roost that night.

Later on, in spring, especially if there is a suitable crop

against the wood, it is a first-class place to set out decoys before the pigeons' bedtime, or even all day long, thereby breaking the normal rules.

I have personally never had a great score on water though I know it can be done. Perhaps there are too many cattle troughs or chalk streams in this area; each reduces the concentration at the dew or other ponds which would otherwise provide the only drinking places. In very dry weather there are a few places on the downs where you can get the birds in either the early morning or late evening. Grain makes them thirsty and water aids their digestion. I make a simple hide which covers the pool, and use only one or two decoys, as this is a case where the picture they expect to see consists of few rather than many birds. Maybe even these are unnecessary, as they are coming for a definite purpose to a small area. Undisturbed, they do not seem to hang about the bar for long. I rather think that a small boy with an air gun would do more damage than a 12-bore. This is certainly one case where a lot of noise does not help. Local knowledge and observation are vital. It will not pay to sit over water without knowing that it is patronized by a large percentage of the local population. The tell-tale signs will be there, feathers, droppings and the marks of feet in the mud at the edge. Perhaps you will be compensated for a poor evening by seeing the other local residents who come to drink. But I am rather glad that there are not many places around here where it is worth going out specially. If I have shot a good number during the day, I rather feel that I prefer the survivors to resume their normal existence without further interference.

I am lucky in that I look after a lot of ground, so if pigeons are in short supply in any area, I can always try another. Not so many others, a fact borne out by the rather sad recurring question asked after almost all lectures 'What do I do if I can't find any definite field? I haven't anywhere else to go, or no transport'. Well, it is impossible to answer this in any helpful manner. If there aren't any pigeons about my old 'picture' won't do much good, you can't conjure them up out of the air. So go home and take it out on the garden!

But if there are some birds about, though not on any particular field then these ideas on advanced decoying are all I can offer to help. They may even solve your problem, as has happened to all of us when birds are feeding over the boundary, where for one reason or another you cannot go. In this case the power of your shot may lift them and may bring them across to you and at least give you some sort of a shoot. But anyway have a go, though, as I have already said advanced decoying works better with a fair number of decoys to start off, I would suggest ten minimum.

MIXED BAG

Roosting

A great deal has been written about shooting pigeons coming in to roost. If, for geographical or time reasons, you cannot use decoys outside the wood as suggested, there seems only one vital factor. You must discover where they are actually roosting in the wood. Local knowledge may help, but the only safe way to find this out is to look for the droppings. I have often been asked by people, 'Come and shoot this afternoon, they are roosting in X wood.' When I asked what time I am to be there, they usually give a time which allows one no chance to search around and decide where to stand. I like to have at least half an hour to sum up the situation and poke about, before any self-respecting pigeon would think of coming in. In the south, pigeons will roost in any favoured type of timber. From where I am writing, within a four-mile radius, they roost year after year in the same places — but in beech, conifers, oak, ash, birch and the 'Hampshire hedge'.

I do not think the wind has as much to do with which wood they choose to roost in as convenience to their present feeding ground. Where they roost in the wood itself is another matter, but even so I do not think the wind plays an all-important part. Provided there is some shelter pigeons, like the cock pheasant, will roost in the same tree, just as we prefer (usually!) to sleep in the same bed.

Roosting on a still day is not very productive; you have to wait until they come within range, as they will almost certainly come in high over the wood and then 'peel off'. A strong wind, however, will channel incoming birds and you must put yourself on this line, preferably somewhat upwind of the main droppings area, so that your shot may make any birds which sit in front of you carry on upwind. But it is usually a question of watching and then moving to the right place — fifteen yards can make all the difference.

Occasionally a 'sitty tree' can be found beside which one can stand. I have already said that I do not like to be tied down to one place while roosting. Until birds show me, I never know exactly where I am going to stand, so I cannot make a hide, and usually stand or sit still until I fire, with my back to a tree. If you do this, pigeons will not see you, but by all means pull a few branches across if you have time. Or wear a mask, though personally I can't stand them. Shooting from platforms can be great sport, but I think only in fairly small woods where the roosting is concentrated. Otherwise a wrong wind can spoil your fun, as you are rather cast.

A somewhat wild dog (like mine!) which will pick up automatically without being bidden is most useful in wood shooting. Simba watches, listens for the crash and off he goes. He returns with the bird, and lays it down, not bringing it to hand unless it is wounded. When I pick up there is a long line of pigeons by my stand and very few left to look for. He seems to be able to remember up to about four, but after that gets a bit muddled.

Just as they prefer certain feeding grounds, year after year, so do pigeons prefer certain woods to roost in, and they keep on trying to come in for a surprisingly long time. I have heard it said that one can only get a good bag if there are a lot of people out. Provided the lone shooter finds the droppings, and places himself near enough the line so that he can move to the right place by observation, he will get a lot of shooting.

Those who shoot too late commit a number of errors. First, they cannot pick up properly, it being too dark to see (and don't forget your decoys outside the wood, if you have been playing the game of catching the early bird home). Secondly, it is much wiser, if you want to shoot the same wood next week, to let the survivors come in unmolested. Last, but certainly not least, you are probably in the wood by courtesy of the owner and, more directly, the keeper. So it is a rather ungrateful act not to stop early enough to allow the pheasants up to roost. Any bangs after this period, when you hear the first cock going up, are liable to arouse misgivings in the breast of the keeper. I don't think pheasants mind much. Some time ago, when I was roosting, a cock pheasant sat on a branch within 20 feet of me, going up very early. Each time I shot a pigeon, he made a gurgling noise, but was rather obviously silent when I missed one. Unfortunately I dropped a bird very nearly on top of him and he flew off loudly protesting at being so rudely ousted from his ring-side seat. But even so, don't spoil your good relations for a few more minutes' shooting. If you have to shoot in the dark, take it out on the duck. You can roost and then flight, if you leave the pigeons early enough and the pond is not too distant. But you have to get a move on.

Roosting shoots by experienced guns can be very successful, if they are well organized and people play the game. This means someone in charge, guns in known roosts and a definite time for the last shot. I almost included 'no anti-aircraft practice', but if your guns are experienced they should certainly know that loose shooting is the surest road to disaster in an organized evening's shoot.

Organized Day Shoots

I have gone a step further than this and organized day decoying shoots with three or four of my friends who know the ropes. Obviously this requires a good deal of local knowledge and preparation, as your guns may be spread out over quite an area. So permission has to be obtained from several farms or different beats. I usually do this in winter on the clover leys, putting a gun on the most favoured field in an area. This year I had to do this on seed rape fields, there being too many of them too close together for me to handle. If the pigeons get fed up with being shot at, and clear off to another area, they are likely to find another gun presenting them with what looks like a nice safe feed and then get a nasty shock. And so they are pushed around, and we have had some nice scores in this way, in the 200–300 class, which is good for winter shooting. The one thing to remember is to leave the woods quiet, at least during the day. All guns should be placed in the open, where pigeons are feeding. Thus, scared birds can return to the woods and sit there until hunger forces them to have another try at finding an undisturbed field. Otherwise, the rules for each gun are exactly the same as if he was on his own.

A point brought out at question time in lectures is the situation where two guns go out together and they find a feeding field but it is only suitable for one hide, or they don't like sharing a hide. In fact one chap gets the shoot, the other is rather out of it. I find exactly the same thing when I take people out, I want them to have the best place, what do I do? The answer is that there is almost always a 'refuge', it might be a secondary feeding place, or it might be a place which is the direct result of the shot. You have to be a little careful of upsetting the return flight to your friend but there is usually somewhere, very often upwind which can result in a sort of merry-go-round. This can only be found by observation but if your friend shoots and pigeons fly to this refuge, you then shoot and so it goes on. Sometimes it takes me an hour to find this place.

Organized day shoots are surely one of the answers for the pigeon shooting clubs. They presumably have the ground, they certainly have the guns and I should have thought they could really go to town at weekends. But some organization is required and a really careful reconnaissance on a Friday is called for, and over a good wide area. That evening the organizer should hold a sort of briefing with members so that each one knows where to go. In this connection my remarks on page 122 on marketing the bag should be noted.

Beech-Mast and Acorns

I have already mentioned that a big beech-mast or acorn year causes much lamenting in the Coats' household. But when permission is given, it can be the greatest fun and you can have all the tame pheasants you want: I'll settle for the pigeons who are, usually, on their best form. Acorns, anyway, seem to make them fat as butter. Perhaps the finest pigeon shooting, and this time I mean the most difficult, is to be had at birds lilting in a high wind, between or over tall oaks or beeches. They are never on an even plane and slide from side to side with the wind. Everything depends on the line of flight. You simply must get on it, and the more decoys the merrier. You can spread the wings of one or two and hang them on the lower branches. Or cut long rods and prop them up with the sharp end under the chin. Throwing works well, and no doubt the lofted decoy, too. Anything to get them to channel to your hide, which does not need to be on a bit of ground covered by acorns or nuts.

You can make big bags this way. 1959, I think, was a big acorn year, and in an area near here, where there are not normally vast numbers of pigeons, I had over 1,000 in four days' shooting, a friend shooting on two of them. Quality-wise, it was, perhaps, as good as I have ever had. Perhaps it is too much to expect pigeons to come back to one strip of beeches because they prefer the mast there to any other, or to one particular oak wood for the same reason. Be that as it may, and I would not like to give an opinion, it is very possible to combine the line of flight with the power of your shot and so bring them up to decoys, which will do the rest.

1968-9 was a terrific year for acorns in this part of the world. After a very wet harvest, when grain shed all over the place, this glut of acorns was almost an embarrassment. One expected to see pigeons on the stubbles, which pro-vided the richest pickings, and indeed in certain areas they were gleaning old barley well into the New Year. I see from my diary that I shot the first clover ley on 12th January. I think a record. But in the oak areas they stuck to the acorns right through February and some of them seemed as keen on them as on the spring drilling.

Keepers found that feeds were virtually useless most of the season the pheasants having a copious supply of food from the fields and woods and this no doubt caused some of the sad tales about straying birds of which one has heard so much.

There is nothing to add to my advice on how to tackle

pigeons on acorns or beech-mast. The line of flight is all important, then by allying the build-up with the power of the shot, you should be able to bring them in.

Training a Dog

I don't pretend to be an expert dog trainer. And judging by the performances (in real life shooting) of some Field Trial competitors I have seen, I don't think I am any exception! Because of my job I have two great advantages over others. All training is the real thing, and I have a good deal of time for one dog only. Above all, I only train my own dogs. I have never used a dummy, except maybe a ball when they were puppies, and at this I am sure all the pundits will raise their hands in horror!

Anyway, I have endeavoured to train my present dog Simba, and his mother before him, to do what I want with pigeons. Simba had his first lesson, watching his mother in action, from a 'Karri-cot'. As he grew bigger, he learned to 'sit' and not to leave the hide until told. I use 'no' to denote any form of denial. Soon, again with the use of the word 'no', he learned not to touch the decoys or go too near a hedgerow in the nesting season. Sometimes there was a runner and sometimes a bird on its back. Perhaps it was the easy way, but for obvious reasons, I would want the runner first, and so would he. Hand signals directed him if there was a choice and one whistle blast would make him stop and look for these directions. Apart from 'no' and his name, the only other word I used in the hide was 'get out' which he knows means 'get out further, look and receive hand signals'. I seem to hear various friends laughing, and I must admit I used other words at poor Simba, and still do, but I think he is used to that by now. But he is at the stage when I can have

70–80 birds out, and can make him pick up the one I require. Rather belatedly, I admit, to save his ageing boss a walk, he is now being taught to drop a pigeon on its tummy (not on its back) in the place I want it, as a decoy. I think we are winning, at least as far as dropping the bird in the right spot is concerned. Unfortunately, it rather depends on which way up the bird is when he picks it up! But the other day he dropped one which fell clean on its back. I said 'no' in a resigned sort of voice, and he gave me a very nasty look and turned it over with his foot. So he knows all right, but does not want to become a circus dog. Anyway, we will persevere.

You might think he would be bored with pigeons. To some extent he is, particularly during the game shooting. But even so, he sits in the hide and watches. I always try to make the hides, even bale hides, so that he can peer out. And you would think that it was the first he ever saw by the way he catches a half-flying runner flat out, and sometimes in mid-air. Feathers don't seem to worry his insides, Heaven knows why, as he must have eaten pounds of them, even though I try and take most of them out of his mouth. There is one thing that I have never been able to make him do, and that is come in at what I think is the easiest entrance to the hide. He likes his own route and sticks to it. He often gets caught out by incoming pigeons when fetching a bird among the decoys. I do nothing, say nothing, just keep still. The chances are that they will come in quite happily, dog or no dog.

When roosting, he is at his best, watches me shoot, waits for the crash and is off. That is what I have taught him to do, and, as I have already mentioned, he brings the birds back and lays them in a trail. I have often thought I had 40 or more down, and yet had only to look

for two or three. The others were all there. Needless to
say, this training is not the best for a covert shoot, and I
have to peg Simba down! But he loves his day away from
the pigeons and will defeat most dogs, especially in water,
which he adores.

Your dog, too, will be a great help out pigeon shooting. But train him, as keepers are understandably averse
to wild dogs coursing all over their beat!

April 1969. So many people kindly ask me about my
'pigeon dogs' at lectures, that I will bore you for a little
about them. We are all a bit older now and not much wiser,
particularly about pigeons. Old Simba died some years
ago, but I have his grand-daughter, Juno II, a yellow bitch
and much beloved. She too is first-class in water. I have
ruined her, by some people's standards, by allowing her to
hunt, but our small shoot about which some of you may
have read in the *Farmer's Weekly*, is too poor to afford
many beaters and anyway I like going with the beat and so
does she. A good deal better than boring old pigeon shooting every day. So she too requires a good peg at covert
shoots but as she is fearfully strong I have taken the advice
of a friend who invented the gadget you can see in the
diagram. This is a large corkscrew. You attach the lead to

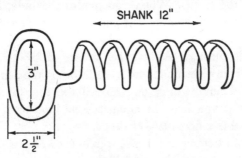

Figure 11

the handle and it is pretty secure in anything like firm ground, though a combination of soft fallow and a strong hare has caused disaster and shame. A local blacksmith, if you can find one in this enlightened age, can make one up on the lines of a rick-sheet peg.

After this digression I am glad to say that Juno's daughter Locket, a very small black bitch, is already showing great promise, and will I hope continue the line which never seems to tire of pigeon feathers.

Safety First

I have heard that a lot of pigeon shooters get careless with their guns. Maybe this is the reason why one reads of more and more accidents, and it is often 'a boy out pigeon shooting'. How much this is the boy's fault, or how much the parents' who never taught him the basic safety rules, I do not know.

Starting from the beginning of a day's pigeon shooting, may I advise you to carry your gun in a slip, preferably with a sling. Place it carefully, last thing, in the car, lest cartridge boxes or large dogs' feet break the stock. Never lean your gun against the car, or a tree for that matter, where it might slip. A dented barrel or damaged stock may be the result. When you get to the hide, lay your gun aside while you build it and set out the decoys. Take the gun out of the slip only when you are ready to shoot, and look through the barrels to see if by chance you have left any cleaning materials lurking therein. I have suggested not holding the gun all the time as it is tiring. But if you leave it against your hide or net, make sure there is a firm place to do so, or make one. Nets have a habit of catching in barrels, top-levers and possibly even triggers, so be doubly careful when using them.

I don't like hearing a 'click' as birds are coming in, if I am in the same hide, perhaps teaching a boy. My father taught me NEVER to put my safety catch off safe until I fired, the whole thing being done in one movement, and he was absolutely right. If the pigeon sees you and you don't fire, can you swear you put the safety back? Remember, it might be in court! I admit that I don't unload my gun when I leave the hide to tidy up. But only when I am alone. I always do so if I have a companion, or if I leave the hide for any length of time, perhaps to go to the car for more cartridges. And I always unload if I get over any obstacle, and I expect others to do the same. My brother once came back to find a small boy in possession of his hide. What's more, he picked up the gun (empty, of course), pointed it at him, and said, 'Halt, I'm a sentry.'

Your hide may be unavoidably sited near a sunken lane or hidden path. Beware of that low pigeon sneaking in that direction; it would be very stupid of someone to be watching you without revealing their presence, but then there are plenty of fools about. You read their obituaries every year, and you must cater for their foolishness! I once had a boy out who used a 20-bore. I caught him, having forgotten his own cartridge bag, filling mine with his 20- and my 12-bore shells. I doubt if he will do it again.

When you pack up, unload your gun and put it in the slip. I put mine in the van last of all, and then I know a sack of 50 pigeons will not be chucked on top of it. And clean it afterwards, properly please, and don't believe all the pundits who say the new wads or powder or whatever it is make cleaning a gun virtually unnecessary!

So for your own safety, and the other fellow's too, which is perhaps more important, don't let careless habits replace your regard for the basic precautions against accidents.

And be merciless to the young, for their own good, and ensure that the old poem 'Never, never let a gun,' etc., is carried out in practice as well as learned by heart.

Everyone who shoots should insure his gun and himself against 'All Risks' including Third Party. The premiums are very reasonable and it is madness not to take out a policy. If I were the 'Powers that be' I would make possession of an insurance policy essential before a gun certificate was issued.

Averages

People often ask me what my average is. Well, of course, it varies with the type of shooting, the weather, and certainly the wind. I don't pretend to hit every bird careering through or over high beeches on a line of flight, in half a gale. Generally speaking, the bigger the bag, the better your average. This should be so, and is so, simply because you cannot have a very big day without decoys, and if you successfully channel pigeons into a killing ground, over decoys, you are inclined to clobber them a bit. And so it should be. Funnily enough, I think my roosting average is as good or better than the decoying score. I like the angle and height they come at, if they are playing the game your way. All in all, over the year, if I fire 100 cartridges I pick up 64 pigeons. I have already said that the farmer (and perhaps the young birds who enjoy the maggots) benefit from another 10 per cent.

I have some friends, a rather select bunch they are (as pigeon shots, I mean!), who come out with me fairly often and whom I call my 1st XI. Sometimes their performance merits demotion to the Junior League, particularly if they have been out on the tiles the night before, but usually they are pretty good, and can at least be relied on to put their hide more or less in the right place, build up their decoy picture, and generally observe hide discipline. One or two have nasty habits. For instance, I have had two bale hides and some brand new nets brewed up by cigarettes carelessly thrown on the ground, presumably as a pigeon came in. And there have been snores on hot afternoons when there was not much doing, but could have been if they had got their guns off.

It is my delight, on being told, 'It's no——use here,' when I don't agree, to take over the hide and by a little noise making and perhaps alteration of decoys, to prove the speaker wrong. But I must admit that with this lot I don't often get the chance, sweet though it is when it does occur! None of them will ever buy this book as they think they know it all, so I can be as rude as I like about them.

Their average will be about one in two (a very few of them better than this, thank goodness, as they use my cartridges!), when things go right and birds are coming in 'at their angle'. And some of them are able to position the decoys so that they can force birds to pass where they want them.

I take out other friends whose average is not so good (some alas, not nearly so good). This is a terrible handicap, because if you cannot hit them and so build up your decoy picture, you lose the vital benefit of the compound interest, and you cannot channel them and so make it much easier for yourself. But sometimes pigeons play ball, with even a few decoys. I had an American out once and started him off with twelve dead birds. He fired 97 cartridges and never touched a feather, though he assured me beforehand that he was quite used to shooting ducks in a 'blind'. I also rather got the impression that the 'limit' in the States (small enough, Heaven knows) was so quickly achieved that it was a terrible expense and bother going out at all, especially after motoring a devil of a long way into the bargain, for a very few minutes' shooting. Anyway, he was delighted and 'had himself a ball', and was in no way put out. On that form the ducks on the Mississippi fly-way, on which I gather he performs, will feel the same way!

I also had another gallant American airman out, who was not a bad shot at all, though how anyone can shoot second barrel with a pump gun defeats me. The first is all right, but the pumping action completely throws you off your swing, as well as being very slow, when you have a quick getaway by *Columba palumbus* to contend with. Anyway, this chap shot 41 birds very nicely, which, with his initial 'stack of deeks', brought his total picture to 53. I counted them when I went to see how he was getting on. I was pleased and so was he. 'How about cartridges?' I asked; 'Oh,' he said, 'I've got plenty in the car.' This was hidden behind a nearby barn. So off I went to my own hide. More bangs, quite a lot more bangs. I picked up and went back, expecting to find a very contented dove-hunter. There were exactly 60 birds in front of him and two very mangled corpses in the hide. 'Gee, Major,' he greeted me, 'after you went, I got another 7 with my remaining shells, then went and got my lunch and some more boxes. But could I hit 'em? Boy, I've fired nearly 75 more and all I get is these two, and look at them. I sure got them all right.'

Well, I was in a hurry, and commiserated and said it was bad luck and perhaps he had a weak eye and the other became master when it got tired. This was a very silly thing to say and frightened the life out of him, and I could see he couldn't wait to get back and have his 'medics' give him a sight test. So we packed up. A week later, I used his hide myself and had a good day. The last 70 shellcases he used, though the same colour green as the Remingtons which he started off with, were marked 'US Federal Reserve. Lethal Ball'. It was lucky we were way out on the downs.

Anyway, pigeon shooting over decoys is a specialized form of amusement and takes practice. So if you go out and shoot one in two, you are doing very well, though at the full price of cartridges, you are still out of pocket even if you get a shilling for a bird. One in three is nice going and perhaps the standard that a careful shot should achieve. After crossing out 75 per cent of all the names on all the lists of so-called expert shots in the country, the remainder might come into this category and could, with reason, tie the label 'Expert Shot' on to their best shooting hats.

If you are a one in four man, that is not quite so good, though many are satisfied with it. Anything over this figure becomes an expensive pastime and the RCS secretaries will not be madly keen to let you have cartridges. But let me assure you that if you obey and follow out the rules and suggestions given in this book, principally those of building up your decoys and hide discipline, the average type of shot you get will become much easier, you will get a lot more shooting, and will quickly become more proficient.

THE BIG DAY

I also called the last chapter in my book *The Amateur Keeper* The Big Day. That was about a small pheasant shoot, this is about a large pigeon shoot; but so many people have asked me about my record day on 10th January, 1962, that I feel I should include the story in this book. This shoot took place on Mr John Rowsell's farm at Stoke Charity, on Lord Rank's estate. The field, sown with S.100 Aberystwyth for pigs, was no stranger to me and in 1961 we killed 800 or more pigeons off it in different shoots, the bale hide used being only a few yards from that used on 10th January. I asked for some fresh bales to be put out and this was done some time in the first week of January.

I set off about 9.30 am, meaning to shoot a clover ley on Lord Rank's Manor Farm at Micheldever. But I found that shooting plans had been changed and so I could not go. I then went to have a look at Mr Rowsell's field, as I knew I could shoot it as the 'first time over' on that particular beat had taken place. This beat was in good form as that particular shoot was also a record for the estate.

At the New Year we had had an intense period of cold and snow and a great many pigeons had died. So I was not expecting an enormous bag and did not have as many cartridges in the van as I usually do. Also my large bag, with about 100 cartridges in it, had got wet the day before and had been forgotten, as it was drying off. Anyway, the field was full of pigeons, and when I had luckily seen beat keeper Mills and got the OK, I realized I was certainly in for a 200 or more day.

It did not take me long to make the hide from the stack of bales and my little picture of ten birds was soon set out. I think I and Simba were in position almost exactly at 11 am: I had a 250 box to start with, and about 25 in my small bag. And then they started and the first half-hour was hot work, with three 25 boxes on the ledge open so that I could load from the top of each to save time and then empty one into the other. I think I picked up twice and got about 70 birds out, very few on sticks, the others simply propped up on the clover. After that it was not necessary, they just came without any lull, from the two main lines of flight mostly; but really there were so many birds in the air over the decoys that I had to keep a tight rein, concentrate and observe a little hide discipline myself! Soon I had to go and get more cartridges, and went to the farm where I got 250. There were 500, but I must say that I thought that 250 would be enough. About half-way through these I had to alter my opinion and realized for the first time that if I went on at that rate I could beat the existing record, though I was not certain what it was — anyway I knew it was not more than 500. I had a short tidy up, though I could not possibly control the feathers, and the place was looking rather like a plucking shed. Then I ran out again at about 2 pm. By this time poor Simba looked as if he was suffering from shell-shock, though he had not had much to do, so I took him back to the car. I then drove to the farm again. The office was shut! I was desperately looking for someone who had a key, when luckily Mr Rowsell's secretary appeared. It was just as well, as I meant to have that other 250 box somehow! On the way back I met Mills, who was watching, and told him I hoped to beat the record. He kindly volunteered to come and spot for me in the hide. This he did, bringing a young labrador with him. By this time, I had lowered the front bale so that we were practically in full view of the birds. It made no difference. The muscles of my thighs were very sore from getting up for certain shots, so I decided to shoot entirely sitting down, which was easy enough as birds were always on the decoys, and some turned back out of lots that had just been shot at. Otherwise, I was not really tired, only anxious to beat the record and have done. They then really went for the decoys, and for about 20 minutes the gun was uncomfortably hot to hold, though I was wearing mittens. It was very hot most of the time, but this period, I think, was the quickest.

After this, Mills did a count of sorts, though it was very difficult, and made the score over 500. By this time it was about 3.15 pm, and there was a slight slackening off. So I decided to enjoy myself, taking everything at any angle, and stop at 4 pm. By this time the word had spread and I fear John Rowsell lost a few man-hours, there being quite an audience.

The last ten minutes were relatively quiet and I stopped shooting at 4 pm and relaxed, though not looking forward to the appalling task of picking up, there being towered birds all over the field. Luckily I was able to borrow a few sacks and drive the van right up to the hide. While I hunted Simba over the field, Mills and a helper put the slain round the hide in piles of 50. Needless to say, I did not hunt any of the surrounding strips, as a second shoot was soon to come and birds would soon be going up to

9. The Author in the bale hide where he shot a record 550 pigeons in a day.

10. A carrion crow which flew over the hide, shooting vermin like this is not only good neighbourliness, it will also keep you on good terms with the keeper.

11. Waiting for roosting pigeons in March. The wood provides enough cover and the large tree gives background. The dog has been trained to retrieve pigeons as they are shot.

12. Pigeon terrine.
Prudence Coats preparing pigeon terrine in her kitchen, and
(*below*) the finished product.

roost. But despite the cannonade several pheasants fed in the field during the day.

We sacked exactly 550 pigeons at the hide. There were 125 cartridges left out of the last 250 box, so I used about 650. Altogether I must have wasted about 40 minutes' shooting time getting cartridges, so my arithmetic (unlike that of Mr William Hickey) makes this one pigeon every 28·5 seconds and one shot every 24 seconds. So I suppose I could have broken 600 carrying the normal amount of cartridges in the van and still leaving enough time to get one lot from the farm. Perhaps the best thing of the day was that Mills only picked up seven the next day when feeding the strips, but the pigs may have had a few.

If you do anything professionally for long enough you will hit the jackpot sooner or later. I expect if you fish a river for many years and in all weathers and get to know the lies and the water really well you may one day kill 50 fish in a day. Anyway, I don't want to do it again and good luck to anyone who breaks this score. But I will lay odds that he will have to use a bale hide to do it!

THE RABBIT CLEARANCE
SOCIETIES AND THE PIGEON

The Rabbit Clearance Societies were first introduced by the Ministry to keep control of the rabbit population, already decimated by myxomatosis.

Groups of landowners, owner farmers and tenants, got together and formed a society, run by a secretary. These societies were limited companies and individually fixed a subscription per acre. Members paid half and the Government went 50/50 with them. The money was mostly used to employ warreners and equipment to deal with the rabbits.

Some time ago, the Ministry and the Federation of Rabbit Clearance Societies Limited decided to incorporate pigeons into the activities of the RCS. Firstly, a farmer could get an allotment of cartridges via the secretary, the quantity being based on his acreage. Again the Ministry paid half the cost and the society half. A farmer could either use the cartridges himself to shoot pigeons, or give or sell them to Expert Shots on a list kept by the local Ministry Pest Officer, who worked closely with the various societies in his county. Nothing was laid down about payment for cartridges and this system is open to abuse, as I have already mentioned.

Secondly, the warreners were employed to poke pigeon nests at stipulated times of the year, which luckily coincided with a period when rabbits were impossible to deal with. Thus their full-time employment was assured.

Let us take a Rabbit Clearance Society of 10,000 acres. It may be made up of one large estate with tenant farmers, or a number of smaller estates either with tenants or privately-owned farms. It does not really matter. What does matter is that the RCS gives its members value for their subscriptions. Quite apart from the bunnies who are dealt with by the warreners, many societies organize as much pigeon-poking as they can in the last week of July and the first week of August, and the second and third weeks of September. One of the chief reasons why large estates are chary of joining RCS is the question of game disturbance. The local keepers are not keen on people walking the hedgerows in July, as they are liable to push young birds off what little headland there is into thick corn, where they may get lost or chilled, especially if it is raining. And in September, when the corn is cut and their outlying feeds are in action, they will want these kept quiet, let alone the feeds in the coverts. It is certainly better if the RCS operators carry guns to shoot the parent pigeons as they come off the nest (or on the nest if you like!), in addition to poking it. But this needs a team of two. Carrying a gun in September, at least, *walking about and banging away with it* is unlikely to endear the pokers to anyone interested in preserving game. I emphasize this, as it is quite different from shooting pigeons from a static hide which in no way worries game.

Now take the pigeon 'damage' year. Let us start on 1st January, on that same RCS ground, all 10,000 acres of it. Pigeons will be eating clover if the weather is not hard, and kale or rape or sprouts, if it is. This will go on through the winter, and we hope that some will be shot roosting as soon as the pheasant shooting is over. About mid-April, after the spring sowing and according to the weather, most intercountry migration or movement ceases. This means that it is unlikely for any one farm or area to get a visitation of fresh birds, though it can happen! So the remaining birds become locals and stay to breed, eating some seed corn in the spring sowing, and then going back to clover. In due course they will do their worst damage in June and July, taking the young kale or brassicas. And then the autumn-sown wheat will suffer when it gets milky and our normal weather and that little extra bit of fertilizer weakens the stalk and lays it nicely for them! Then our RCS pokers come into action and do what they can, destroying eggs or young and perhaps shooting the adults as well. Those they do not kill will surely lay again and, we hope, will not be missed next time over, which should be six weeks from the first operation. Meanwhile, more wheat or barley is being eaten, and in due course the young survivors fly off, probably in late September or October, by which time the warreners will be back on rabbits. No one (except me!) will worry too much about flocks of young birds on the stubbles. 'They are doing no harm' and they are quite likely to go elsewhere and be replaced by others. But they must stay and in due course start on the clover, and be joined by other wanderers seeking pastures new. And so we start all over again.

The point I want to make is this: a RCS is doing its members lots of good as regards rabbits, but it is a hard fact that it may do them little good by nest-poking alone. For early nests and adults, there is a short-term benefit while the harvest remains uncut. As I have already said, any area is at the mercy of a visiting flock from October to certainly the middle of April, and valuable crops like young kale or seed all come at a time when pigeon-poking is impossible, and the last migrant arrivals have become local residents. So unless far more societies in the country poke pigeon nests properly, and so kill potential breeders, individual RCS pigeon-poking activity must be on a purely 'for the good of the community as a whole' basis. Too many people believe that by destroying five nests in the Water Spinney, they are going to have that fewer pigeons on their farm in the future. Come October, this is simply not so and it may be an expensive delusion to labour under, when the cost of poking a nest is 1s 6d. Someone will benefit, certainly. The old 'organized' roosting shoots were maybe a waste of money, partly through abuse and bad organization; but every pigeon killed was one less to breed!

However, the 44 per cent of agricultural ground and woods covered by the present RCS is a very good start, considering that they are only four years old. One might think that about a third of the country's pigeon population was in jeopardy. But how many actually do their poking programme properly?

I see that the Ministry of Agriculture's Advisory Leaflet 165, *The Wood Pigeon*, says that two men can poke 80 acres of average nesting habitat twice, that is, in the two specified periods already mentioned. All told, this requires 320 man-hours based on the assumption that two man-hours per acre are required.

I shoot less often than I used to, but still kill about 12,000 to 14,000 pigeons a year. Say I shoot four days a week, say 200 times a year. This means I average 60–65 birds a day. Based on six hours' shooting time per day (you won't get more off one particular field), 320 man-hours comes to 53 shooting days. Let us say 50. Therefore I would kill 3,000 pigeons (50 ×60) on an average in the same number of man-hours as the pokers. These birds would be adults, if you like to take a vital period starting on 20th May and going right through to the end of July. This covers your 50 days' shooting; but you can cover a longer period if you shoot less often. 3,000 pigeons shot at this time will surely save a lot of young and valuable crops, and you kill a high proportion of the breeding stock at the same time. Turn that kale or other valuable crop into money and then see if you do not agree that a pigeon shooter 'on call' might not be a good insurance policy. If those pokers can kill 3,000, or a potential of 3,000, in 80 acres of woodland, they are better men than I, and I don't care how high the nest concentration is!

I do not know what proportion out of a total of £450,000 is allocated to the pigeon-poking or cartridge side of RCS. I believe RCS as a whole costs the Government £218,000 and the remainder is expense born by the societies themselves. Anyway, it costs 1s 6d to poke a nest. Certainly on my yearly average of 64 pigeons for every 100 cartridges (and with the 10 per cent I lose it is more like 70), I can kill the old birds, and so prevent them breeding at all, cheaper than this, particularly with cartridges supplied through RCS. The above figures are taken from the March issue of *The Federation of Rabbit Clearance Societies Limited Newsletter*.

I have always believed since creating my professional pigeon shooter job twelve years ago, that the place to kill pigeons was 'on the crops where they were doing the damage, all the year round'. This is practical and perfectly possible to achieve. The migratory habits of the pigeon require someone full-time 'on call' to save your clover and green stuff in winter, and above all to thin out the local inhabitants, and at the same time save the young and valuable crops in June and July. Ideally the local population should be so reduced by the time the corn is ripe that there should be little trouble. And there are certain areas which I look after where this very thing happens. No one expects to kill the last pigeon. Movement in the winter months prevents that. But that is surely the best reason for having a man 'on call' as a form of insurance. Killing pigeons by decoying saves the farmer crops and money, and he should surely be prepared to help pay for it.

Several times in the past few years I have suggested to the Ministry of Agriculture that they might consider appointing a token number of professional pigeon shooters; to start with, one in each of the worst hit counties. I even offered to train them. But I was always told that there were no funds. But at least another objection has now been disposed of by the introduction of RCS. The Ministry always said that farmers should pay for the protection of their own crops, with which sentiment I heartily agree. Some societies are now in a position to consider financing the appointment of a full-time pigeon shooter.

To start with, I would like to see one man trained for each of the following counties: Hampshire, Wiltshire, Berkshire, Bedfordshire, Huntingdonshire, Essex, Suffolk, Norfolk and Lincolnshire. Say nine in all, and if any other county feels hurt and thinks that they should be included there is room for one more to make the ten originally suggested! When trained, these men would operate on call in their county, their pay being partly provided by the RCS and partly by the Government, on much the same lines as the present set-up. To start with, they might operate only on RCS ground, though this has snags, as I am all for killing pigeons where you find them, and it would be a pity if a man was not allowed to go on a non-member's ground where there was sure to be a large concentration!

But this might be an incentive to wavering farmers to join the society, particularly those who had much pigeon trouble but whose bunnies were well in hand. These men would all have to have a van.

If it worked, the natural outcome of this pilot scheme is to have these men train others, drawn locally, and so form a small 'fire brigade' in each county, perhaps under the direction of the local Pest Officer. Apart from local knowledge being invaluable for pigeon shooting, local people are much more likely to be accepted than strangers. Once owners, agents, tenants and keepers get to know you and are certain that you will play the game, the rest is comparatively easy. And as I have already said, shooting pigeons over decoys in a static hide does not disturb game.

I get many letters from people wishing to become professional pigeon shooters, so that there would be no lack of suitable applicants who would be only too willing to take up such a job.

In view of the millions lost annually by farmers to pigeons, it is surely not too much to suggest that such a scheme, based on successful experience over a number of years, should at least be considered. I have made an approach to the Federation of Rabbit Clearance Societies, and hope that in due course something may come of it.

If only we could increase the popular demand for pigeons as food, this would be one of the best ways of reducing the pigeon population, as happened during the war. The incentive to shoot then rises just about as fast as the price you get increases! The French and most continentals love them, even at 7s 6d as they are in Paris. (Alas for those who think they will pull a fast one on Coats and export to France. I can just see the arithmetic humming, but the French won't let them in just now.

Maybe the Common Market if it comes will alter this, but you will have to be very much on the ball to defeat me!) The Americans revere squab, and it always infuriates me that you get less for a young pigeon in this country than for an old one. All other 'young' are much more expensive. Young pigeons, including Stock Doves, are simply classified 'small' by the market. Pigeons are excellent if you cook them right. (See last chapter for the excellent recipes dreamed up and practised by my wife.) But if the Government could only find some way of processing pigeons or some means of selling them, it would help the financial side of my scheme very much. The mere fact that people cannot afford to shoot pigeons as they cannot sell them, has a direct bearing on the present population; and if there were many professional shooters, on the present market basis, they might have to bury a lot as they could not get rid of them otherwise. Thus they would be entirely dependent on their salary, which in turn would cost both the RCS and the Government more.

We hear reports of narcotics experiments. A pigeon is a tough creature and needs a lot of dope to put him under. More than a rook, if French experiments are anything to go by. Any such dope would surely have to be selective. If small birds or game were rendered unconscious or killed, I think the public would find it difficult to accept such a scheme; and anyway, I believe that an Act of Parliament would have to be passed to permit it. At long last we seem to have got rid of the poisonous seed dressings which were such a menace to all wild life. Personally I and many others wish that the present 'understanding' might become law. And in Scotland I am told that the position is still unsatisfactory. I believe the Ministry of Agriculture are experimenting with doping or poisoning peas.

Personally I can't see much difference between toxic seed corn and toxic peas put out on purpose, though these are supposedly too large for a small bird to swallow. I always thought peas split! It is apparently done on a ley in winter, as they have found out that they got too many pheasants and partridges on stubble. As it was, one in four perished. Apparently the stuff will only be administered on licence by Ministry of Agriculture staff. My information is very scanty, but one must ask certain questions. If anyone picked up a pheasant or partridge or pigeon which had died from eating too much of the stuff, would it be fit to eat? If not, and the bird was sold, the buyer being ill as a result, who would be responsible? The seller, the farmer or landowner on whose ground the poisoning took place, or the Ministry? If they are toxic, how are they collected or buried? Can one be sure that a pea or two taken might not allow a bird to fly off and be found later.

What effect does the drug have on the breeding systems of birds who eat a little but survive? As I have written elsewhere, my friends in the USA Wild Life Service felt that this was the greatest danger of all, hidden as it was, in the use of toxic seed dressings. Is there any such danger here?

What happens to the cat, dog or fox which eats a bird which has died? What about their reproductive organs, if they were to eat a lot or to continue doing so over a period?

There is a great danger of such a scheme wrecking the sale of pigeons throughout the country. At various times over the past few years the sensational press have only to mention the fact that pigeons have been found dead, and the sales go down and have virtually stopped for a period. If doping did stop the sale of pigeons, and I am quite sure that it would in the same way as the public reacted to myxomatosis, then there would be no alternative to doping. I simply couldn't go out and shoot pigeons and bury them. I would stop shooting and get another job.

Apart from the obvious poaching possibilities, if pigeons aren't fit for sale after a pea or two, then presumably game are not either. This will be charming for many people who rely on the sale of game to run their shoots. Can one see the cunning hand of the 'Anti's' in this? How far have they permeated the Ministry? A nice painless(?) death for a naughty pest which eases their conscience? And then the ramifications; people won't shoot pigeons, won't shoot game, if they can't sell it, so many people can't afford to grow game or shoot pigeons, and, as I have said, the gilt goes right off the gingerbread if you shoot only to bury. Far-fetched perhaps, but I don't know. After shooting my big bag of pigeons earlier this year, the publicity resulted in my receiving one or two unsigned letters which shook me, so virulent was their tone. Anyhow, it is all very disturbing. Right or wrong, I hated myxy and the seed-dressing business. And I now hate the idea of further tampering with nature, particularly when I believe that it is quite unnecessary. Shooting pigeons over decoys is the best answer, at least until the RCS pigeon-poking activities are on a far larger scale. Unfortunately, there are certain people in exalted positions in the Ministry of Agriculture who do not agree with me or their own men on the ground, who think as I do. I was shown a letter at the Longleat Game Fair by a man from Dorset who had complained that he could not get cartridges from his local RCS for pigeon shooting. This letter said that 'experience has shown that shooting pigeons does not materially reduce their numbers'. On the present basis, where I and possibly one or two others are the only so-called professionals in the whole country, he is dead right. How on earth can one or two people make an impression? Most other people have jobs and can only function at weekends. But otherwise this statement is utter nonsense. Expert pigeon decoying can and does vastly reduce the pigeon population, and all the county Pest Officers who I have met agree with me. At least their feet are firmly on the ground! I believe that if professional pigeon shooting could be established in a reasonable way throughout the country, there would be no need for any other method of control. Some of the facts and figures I have quoted may give rise to the question as to whether money now being spent, either by the Government or by RCS themselves, is being put to the best use.

In *The Federation of Rabbit Clearance Societies Limited Newsletter* of March 1962, page 3, Mr R. H. M. Robinson, Chairman of the South-East Essex RCS, is quoted as follows: '. . . one of the secrets of success in operating a Rabbit Clearance Society was to be able to find out where there was trouble as soon as it occurred, and to be in a position to assign operators to deal with the trouble immediately. In his Society the Secretary at this office received telephone calls from members and assigned the operators to particular jobs by telephone. In this way the Society tried, and nearly always succeeded in providing a twenty-four-hour service to all members. The work was shared out amongst the operators by the senior operator in consultation with the Secretary. All the operators visited the Headquarters together once a week, where they met the Secretary and Chairman and exchanged information on conditions and numbers of rabbits and any other trouble in the area. Close liaison was maintained with Pest Officers of the Ministry of Agriculture who check the area covered by the Society regularly. This helped the Society by pin-pointing any troubles which might arise through rabbits infiltrating from non-members' land over which the Society had no control. The management of the Society looked for information as to areas where the rabbits were returning from three independent sources — reports from the Ministry, individual members, and the Society's operators.'

Mr Robinson was talking about rabbits. With only a few additions or alterations, he could easily have been talking of pigeons.

It is now six years since I wrote this. I must say straight away that I find it difficult to add materially to it, I believed then that the best way to control pigeons in this country was by regular shooting by experts over decoys. I still believe it, only more so than ever.

I have several good friends who also presumably believe that I am doing a good job, or they would not either employ me or anyway give me some help in cartridges. I have already explained that all the year round pigeon shooting can and does keep pigeons down and in control over a given area. Let me once again point out the fact that most people seem to find hardest to grasp. This is that from late April or whenever the sowing virtually ceases there is no migratory movement, or very little. Thus pigeons become parochial and stay to breed. In May, June and July the vulnerable and expensive young crops come up. So by killing the local population on these crops I not only destroy the breeding population and so keep numbers down, but I also protect these valuable crops from damage. This must surely be a worthwhile contribution and worth some form of remuneration, provided always that one is on call any day, like a fire brigade.

At other times of the year, notably the winter months, one can only control pigeons at the same time as reducing their numbers and keeping them off whatever cropping is on their menu. Migration is taking place and you never know when an area will get a new wave. But even then pigeons can do a lot of damage particularly in hard weather and the full-time pigeon shooter is surely worth a little help for his time spent, often in intense cold trying to protect the farmer's livelihood.

Perhaps we are a little nearer to achieving something. I had the honour to be guest speaker at the Federation of Rabbit Clearance Societies Conference at Harrogate in 1968. Several Secretaries supported my idea of having a full-time professional on the books of the society. Indeed two societies, including one in Northumberland, on my advice had already taken the plunge, and members were very pleased with the results. But the main stumbling block is still the question of finance. If the Ministry are willing to pay half the warrener's wages, I don't quite see why they are unwilling to do the same with a professional pigeon shooter, if the pigeon is doing the damage they say he is to the farming economy. I mean, is the pigeon on the same menace basis as the rabbit or not?

But I do indeed see and agree with their contention that the farmer should pay for the protection of his own crops and here is the rub. The great majority of farmers are not willing to do this as they would have to for the services of a vet. They regard pigeon shooting as a 'perk' and unfortunately, as it is the only sport that many people can afford or can get, there are plenty who will in fact do it for nothing. There are other points which should be noted. At the conference I gave my reasons for believing that Rabbit Clearance Society cartridges should be distributed to regular pigeon shooters by the secretary, not by the farmers. As I have mentioned elsewhere, pigeons are no respecter of boundaries for one thing, and this method cuts out the difficult members for another. Let the RCS secretary get the money from them, with their subscription. Another point at issue is the charming way in which farmers or indeed the secretary of a Rabbit Clearance Society will offer you RCS cartridges at, say, half price. You know that the Government pays 50 per cent of the cartridge cost. If you pay the other half, then once again the farmer has his crop protected for nothing. I spelled this one out in words of one syllable at Harrogate, and at all the lectures I have given, and I think a lot of those present had not thought of it in this way.

I make no apologies for harping on this theme as to me it appears only sensible and just that some form of payment should be made to regular and planned pigeon destruction. And it should be noted that the cost of pest destruction is a perfectly legitimate item to be set against the profit and loss account in the farm ledger. It is this issue which has plagued me most since this book was first published. The future of pigeon shooting in this country must surely depend on some form of cooperation between those who do it regularly and those who benefit.

Pigeon shooting clubs can make a great contribution to making life uncomfortable for the pigeon. Last year I got into trouble with the secretary of perhaps the most prominent club. 'Why are professionals necessary?' he said, 'why not members of the Club'? The answer to that is that if club members can function regularly all through the year on weekdays, rain or shine, it is fine and dandy.

Knowledge and skill, are all very well, but the fire
brigade theme of always being on call must be the final
yardstick.

There has been much talk and controversy about the
doping of pigeons, predominantly on brassicas, with tick
beans coated with alpha chloralose. From conversations
with Ministry officials on 'ground level', it appears that
the Ministry did not really want to carry out the Bedfordshire trials (shunted from Lincolnshire owing to foot and
mouth), as they had enough evidence already that the
scheme did not really work, besides being very costly. But
they were pressurized into doing the trials by a group of
influential NFU members. These trials were conducted and
paid for by the Ministry. Figures given showed that they
could kill a certain number of pigeons though the numbers
of other birds, both game and song affected seemed a little
vague. I know a little bit about alpha chloralose, it is
powerful stuff. The French found that it took more dope to
knock out a wood pigeon than it did a rook or a cock
pheasant. We were told that small birds would not eat the
beans as they were too big. But they would surely peck
them as the tits do the groundnuts which I put out for them
in a bag. The Eley Game Research Station at Fordingbridge conducted a trial not so long ago in which they hid
or planted dead pheasants or partridges on a given area.
They then got some keepers, who presumably know how
to use their eyes, gave them a time limit and told them to
look. I believe they only found about 30 per cent. It must
be very difficult surely to conduct a proper search in a
30-acre field of brussels sprouts.

As regards the cost, if people would pay me to shoot
a pigeon the same price as the Government paid to dope a
bird with alpha chloralose, I would be taking a gun in a

good grouse syndicate without much trouble! Now that the new licence agreement stipulates that farmers must pay for the dope and the labour, I wonder if the gentlemen in the NFU will be quite so keen. I realize how maddening it must be for a brussels sprouts grower, for example, to see a valuable crop being attacked. But I assure them and at my last visit to Lincolnshire have offered to prove my words, that, with the help of bale hides a considerable number of birds can be killed and the gun acts at the same time as a lethal scarecrow. If the crop is so valuable it is surely worthwhile paying a little 'insurance money' to the pigeon shooter. And believe me, the cost to the grower will be far less than that entailed by the doping method.

Another development has made the use of narcotics, with their possible side effects on game a highly undesirable method of controlling pigeons. This is the happy fact that an export market in pigeons has developed and for the first time since the war the price of pigeons now makes it worthwhile to shoot them. When talking early this year to members of two rabbit clearance societies in Lincolnshire the chairman and secretary between them very sensibly asked the buyer of a local export firm to attend the meeting. I was able to introduce him and tell the members that by pooling their bags and making up a total which made it worth his while to collect, they could get a very reasonable price. Now this was in one of the areas where the doping trials were to have taken place. It was made very clear to me by members that any further trials would not be welcome, if only for the simple reason that you cannot expect to sell possibly contaminated birds, whether pigeons or game. I put this some time ago to the National Federation of Wholesale Poultry Merchants, and they showed me a letter from the Ministry which in essence said that the consumption taken by means of the stupefying bait need present no cause for alarm. It also said that the use of this technique offers little risk to game birds. Well, I put this to the meeting and also to the exporter present and 80 per cent of those present said they would not think of eating a bird which had dope in it. The exporter said that he sincerely hoped his customers in Europe would not hear of this possibility. I must agree with this representative group of countrymen, I don't think there is any real argument about it.

Anyway one can only hope that this price will continue. I have asked the National Federation of Wholesale Poultry Merchants to be very careful not to flood the market as they did two years ago. It will be a help to the exporters, who may well make these pigeons oven-ready if everyone opened the crops of pigeons shot, particularly after they have been on greenstuff, otherwise the crop ferments and makes a nasty smell which can affect the flesh. And of course it will now be even more vital to de-fly them, as explained earlier in this book.

I can't help fearing that some farmers will be delighted at this new price, albeit it is only for export, as they can now quote it as a further excuse for not paying for the protection of their livelihood, knowing perfectly well that the poor pigeon shooter will go anyway. You can't win, I know, but that doesn't make it right.

I wish the British housewife would get it into her foolish head that pigeon pie is not the only possible way of cooking them, and not very often at that. We never get tired of pigeon, the fact that there is an export market means that some people respect it for the excellent table bird it is. If you will look at the next chapter you will see some of the answers provided by my wife.

PRACTICAL AND UNUSUAL
PIGEON RECIPES

By Prudence E. Coats

The first thing people always say to me when they hear that my husband shoots pigeons for a living, is 'Don't you get absolutely sick of pigeon?' The answer is, emphatically 'No!' I think that cooked properly, with intelligence and a little imagination, they can be a gourmet's dish. The other remark they generally make is 'I suppose you roast them, or make pigeon pie?' The answer again is 'No!' Whilst I think both these ways of cooking pigeon are excellent, they nevertheless come rather low down on my list.

Another widely believed fallacy is that pigeons need long, slow cooking to tenderize them. Of course, for some recipes such as casseroles, this is an essential part of the drill, but on the whole I believe they need cooking in much the same way as steak — quickly for a few minutes to seal in the juices, and then a moderate heat for a few more minutes to finish them off.

I suppose that as I have to deal with so many pigeons, I have become rather extravagant in my method of preparing them. Not for me (or very rarely) the ritual of plucking, drawing and trussing. When my husband comes in after a big shoot and says. 'There are about 20 or 30 thin pigeon that will have to be used up' (this usually happens in

January or February when they have been on kale or rape for some time), then when time is short one has to find the quickest way of dealing with them. This is very simple indeed, and is particularly suitable for people living in small flats in towns who have nowhere to pluck birds — and I must say that of all the feathers I have had to deal with pigeon are the worst, and seem to penetrate everywhere!

You first of all place the pigeon on the kitchen table with the vent facing you. Take a very sharp knife and slit through the feathers and skin between the thighs and body, then draw the knife round the end of the breast-bone, above the vent. Now pull the skin right over the breast as far as the crop. It will come off exactly like a glove. Now take your sharp knife and slice the meat off either side of the breast. With a little practice the whole operation should take only two or three minutes, and in no time at all you have a nice mound of pigeon breasts awaiting your favoured treatment.

The other method of preparation is the normal one. First pluck your bird (if you don't want the feathers to fly all over the place, dip the bird in hot water first and pluck it into the sink). Now cut off the head and feet (unless you fancy the feet left on, which I don't), slide the skin down the neck and cut it off as close to the body as you can, and work the crop loose. Take your sharp knife in the right hand and with your left thumb feel for the pointed end of the breast-bone, and pull it upwards, thus making the skin taut above the vent. Make a horizontal slit in this, hold the bird up with your left hand, insert two fingers of your right hand and just loosen the entrails, shake, and the whole thing will come out quite easily. Pick out the liver, heart and gizzard, and reserve for stock or sauce, as you wish.

Fold the wings under the back, press the legs back, run a skewer through the bird and tie down the legs in the normal way, after sprinkling the inside of the bird with salt and pepper, or filling with stuffing.

The following are a number of recipes which can be done very quickly and require only pigeon breasts, so the first method of preparation is the most suitable. If you have a deep freeze, then it will pay you to have one or two cartons of breasts, whole, and ready cut-up or minced. Minced pigeon is excellent for Bolognese or Milanese sauce with spaghetti, and is widely used for this purpose in Italian restaurants.

GRILLS

GRILLED PIGEON
Four servings

8 pigeon breasts (4 birds), 1oz butter, Lawries' Season-All Salt, soya sauce, redcurrant jelly, ground black pepper, cream or top of milk

Cut the 8 pigeon breasts into cubes about 1 inch square. Melt butter in bottom of grill pan, after removing wire grid. When it begins to turn brown, throw in the pigeon and shake around so that each piece becomes coated with butter. Now add a good dash of soya sauce and a tablespoonful of redcurrant jelly, and season well. Mix together and place under a very hot grill for a few minutes until the jelly begins to caramelize, remove, turn heat down to moderate, add a dash of cream and scrape the pan well so that the sauce looks coffee coloured, replace under the grill for another 5 minutes. The meat should still be faintly pink inside. Serve with rice or mashed potato.

CURRIED PIGEON
Four servings

8 *pigeon breasts*, 1 *oz butter*, *hot curry powder*, *soya sauce*, *mango chutney*,
  cream or top of milk

Prepare pigeon as above. Melt butter in grill pan, add pigeon cubes, curry
powder to taste, a dash of soya sauce and a tablespoonful of mango chutney
juice. Follow above method of cooking. We prefer Bolst's Sweet Lucknow
Chutney, and Hot Mango Kasondie or Ranji's Hot Curry Powder, but these
are not always easy to obtain.

DEVILLED PIGEON BREASTS

Four servings

8 *pigeon breasts*, 2 *oz butter*, 1 *heaped tsp flour*, 1 *heaped tsp dry mustard*, 1 *tsp*
  demerara sugar, *Worcester sauce*

Soften the butter, and make a paste with the other ingedients, adding a good
dash of Worcester sauce last of all. Spread this mixture over the pigeon
breasts and lay in the bottom of the grill pan. Place under a moderate heat
for about 7–10 minutes. Turn and baste when the paste begins to bubble and
turn brown, and cook for another 5 minutes. Serve on toast or with mashed
potato.

PATÉS

RICH PIGEON PATÉ
Makes approximately 1¼ lb

10 *pigeon breasts*, ¼ *small onion*, 1 *tsp mixed herbs (including basil and rosemary*
  if possible), ½ *oz streaky bacon*, 4 *oz lard*, 4 *oz butter*, ½ *port glass wine*, *sherry*,
  brandy or whisky, *salt*, *ground black pepper*, *garlic (optional)*, 6 *crushed*
  juniper berries (optional)

Prepare breasts as above. 'Melt' bacon and onion in butter and lard in a
thick frying pan, so that they are cooked but not browned. Turn up heat and
sauté the pigeon breasts. This should take only a few minutes, and they
should be fairly pink inside. Remove from the pan and put aside. Add the
herbs, seasoning (plenty of black pepper) and wine to the butter and let it
bubble for a few seconds. Add to the pigeon and place in a liquidizer until

well pounded. (If you do not possess one, simply pass the meat through a fine mincer and then beat in the butter and wine with a fork.) Put into an earthenware dish or terrine and cover with melted butter. Place in a refrigerator. Serve well chilled with piping hot toast.

PIGEON PATÉ WITH ORANGE

10 *pigeon breasts, ½ small onion, pinch mixed herbs, ½ oz streaky bacon, ¼ lb butter, ½ tsp finely grated orange rind, ½ port glass orange juice, ½ port glass sherry or madeira, ½ cup aspic jelly, salt, pepper.*
Follow method in above recipe, but instead of pouring melted butter over the pâté allow it to get quite cold, then lay paper-thin halved slices of orange down the centre of the dish, slightly overlapping, then pour over the aspic jelly and allow to set.

PIGEON MOULD

10 *pigeon breasts, ¼ lb sausage meat, ¼ lb chopped bacon, 1 breakfast cup brown stock, ¾ oz gelatine, 1 port glass red wine, 1 tsp mixed herbs, pepper, salt, garlic (optional), 3 hard-boiled eggs*
Follow previous recipes, but when you remove the sautéd sausage and pigeon meat, pour in the red wine and let it bubble; then add the stock in which you have dissolved the gelatine. (Reserve a little of this for glazing.) Pulverize the meat and liquid in liquidizer, or mince finely. Half fill a terrine or loaf tin with the mixture, place the three eggs lengthwise down the centre, and cover with remainder of mixture. Leave to set and get cold, then turn out and glaze with the rest of the stock and gelatine. Serve with salad.

TERRINE OF PIGEON

10 *pigeon breasts, ¼ lb pigs' liver, ¼ lb belly of pork, ¼ lb streaky bacon, ½ glass cheap brandy, pinch thyme, bay leaves, 1 thick slice of white bread soaked in milk, 2 eggs*
Slice 5 pigeon breasts very thinly into long strips and marinade with brandy, peppercorns, sliced onion, carrot and a 'bouquet garni' for 2–3

hours. Meanwhile mince together the rest of the pigeon breasts, liver, pork and bacon, leaving one or two rashers of bacon as a garnish. Now remove the strips of pigeon breast from the marinade. Discard the onion, carrot and bouquet garni. Mix the liquor from the marinade with the minced pigeon, liver, pork and bacon, add the thyme, seasoning (garlic), bread and eggs. Fill a straight-sided earthenware dish or terrine with alternate layers of minced mixture and pigeon strips, ending with a layer of strips nicely arranged so that they are just overlapping. Lay two rashers of bacon, and two bay leaves on top and cover tightly with aluminium foil. Stand in a roasting tin and fill half-way up the terrine with boiling water. Cook in a moderate oven for 1½–2 hours. Leave to get quite cold, then pour off the juice which will have formed, strain, heat, and dissolve in it a heaped tea-spoonful of gelatine, pour back over the terrine and leave to set. Serve either as a first course, with toast, or as a main course with salad.

These four pâtés will all freeze well, but if you intend to do this they should be made in an oblong loaf tin. Omit the hard-boiled eggs from the pigeon mould, as they go black if frozen. Remove pâtés from deep freeze 24-hours before you intend to use them, and allow to thaw out naturally.

PIES

Six servings

PIGEON AND MUSHROOM PIE

10 *pigeon breasts, 1 small onion, good pinch mixed herbs, 1 oz streaky bacon, 1 tbsp redcurrant jelly, 1 port glass red wine, ¼ lb mushrooms, 1 tbsp flour, 1 oz butter, ½ pt stock (or chicken bouillon cube), flaky or short crust pastry*

Cut pigeon breasts into 1 inch cubes, chop onion and bacon. Sauté the sliced mushrooms in butter, add flour and make a bechamel sauce with the stock. Add pigeon and other ingredients and cook slowly in a tightly covered pan for 1¼ hours. Cool. Fill a large pie-dish with this mixture and cover with flaky pastry. Place in a hot oven for 15 minutes, then reduce to moderate and continue cooking for another 35 minutes. Any surplus filling can be made into a smaller pie to be eaten cold, or put in the deep freeze.

PIGEON PUDDING
Four servings

6 *pigeon breasts, ½ lb ox kidney, 1 small onion, pinch mixed herbs, 1 tsp red currant jelly, stock, 6 crushed juniper berries (optional), suet crust.*

Cut up pigeon breasts and kidney and roll in seasoned flour. Line a pudding basin with suet crust and fill with pigeon, kidney, chopped onion and juniper berries. Fill half-way up with stock and cover with suet crust. Steam for 3 hours. When serving add more hot stock if too dry. (Juniper berries are obtainable at any herbalist or Health Food Shop.)

CASSEROLES

SALMI OF PIGEON
Six servings

3 *whole roast pigeon, 1 tbsp redcurrant jelly, 1 glass port or red wine, ¼ lb button mushrooms, 2 oz butter, 2 tbsp flour, 1 pt stock, 2 finely chopped shallots, 1 tsp tomato purée, salt and pepper*

Cut meat off the cold roast pigeons, which should be rather underdone. Make stock with the carcasses. Melt the butter, add the flour and make a brown roux. Gradually pour in the stock, add the jelly, port, shallot, tomato purée and seasoning and simmer for 1½ hours, or until well reduced. Throw in the sliced mushrooms and cook for another 5 minutes. Draw pan to the side of the stove, and add the pigeon meat. Heat through in the sauce, but on no account allow to boil or the meat will be tough.

PIGEON WITH RED WINE, ONIONS AND RAISINS
Eight to ten servings

6 *pigeons, 4 large Spanish onions, 1 handful stoned raisins, 1 bottle cheap red wine, salt and pepper*

Peel and slice onions into thick rings. Place in bottom of a large saucepan. Place the plucked and trussed pigeons on top of the onions. Season well with salt and pepper, throw in a handful of raisins and pour in ½ the bottle of wine. Drink the rest! Cover tightly and simmer *gently* for 2–3 hours. Remove pigeons on to a dish and keep warm. Thicken the sauce and add a few drops of gravy browning.

This recipe was invented by a friend of ours in his bachelor days, and is especially recommended for grass widowers or lone pigeon shooters!

PIGEON 'GUIDWIFE'

3 or 4 pigeon, 2 large onions, chutney, stock, seasoning
Chop the onions up roughly and brown them well in a large, thick frying pan. Now brown the pigeon, and place them in an earthenware or cast-iron casserole. Surround with the fried onion, spread chutney thickly over the pigeons' breasts, season well and pour in a cupful of stock. Cover tightly and place in a moderate oven for 2 hours, basting occasionally.

ROASTS

PLAIN ROAST PIGEON WITH BACON AND REDCURRANT JELLY

4 to 6 pigeon, 1 tbsp redcurrant jelly, 2 rashers bacon per bird, butter, stock, flour seasoning
Pluck, draw and truss the birds. Place giblets in a small saucepan with some water and bring to simmer. Pre-heat oven to 425°, and melt a knob of butter or margarine in the roasting pan until it is sizzling but not coloured. Place pigeons in pan and cover breasts with 2 rashers of bacon each. Leave for 15 minutes, then reduce heat to 350° for 1 hour. Baste *frequently*. Remove pigeons from pan and place on croutons of toast or fried bread. Sprinkle in a little flour and swill round with some of the stock from the giblets. If liked a little port or red wine can be added.

Allow half a bird per person.

ROAST PIGEON AND ORANGE

As above, but place some thinly peeled orange rind inside each bird. When making the gravy add a glass of orange juice, some finely grated orange peel and a tablespoonful of Escoffier Cumberland sauce. Serve with home-made or bottled Cumberland sauce.

STUFFINGS

CHESTNUT AND MUSHROOM STUFFING

1 *lb chestnuts or* 1 *tin whole unsweetened chestnuts,* ¼ *lb mushrooms, butter, parsley, chopped fried bacon*

Peel and cook chestnuts until tender, and chop up roughly. If you wish to avoid burning your fingers, use a tin of whole unsweetened chestnuts. Fry chopped bacon and sliced mushrooms, then mix together with the chestnuts and a sprinkling of breadcrumbs to bind it together. Season well with salt and black pepper.

CRANBERRY STUFFING

1 *packet cranberries,* 1 *small onion, seasoning, breadcrumbs*

Chop onion finely and cook in a very little water until soft. Mix together with the whole cranberries, seasoning and breadcrumbs. Serve cranberry jelly as an accompaniment. Cranberries are difficult to come by, but can usually be bought at any first-class greengrocer around Christmastime. They come in date boxes under the name of 'Tryphena'. Otherwise they can be bought frozen. The only make I have come across is the American 'Oceanspray'.

HERB STUFFING

1 *breakfast cup breadcrumbs,* 1 *small onion,* 1 *lemon, chopped marjoram, parsley and thyme, salt, ground black pepper.*

Prepare onion as above, but cook in half a cup of water. Mix together with the breadcrumbs. Add a squeeze of lemon juice, ½ tsp finely grated lemon rind and the rest of the ingredients. Ordinary dried mixed herbs can be used if the others are unobtainable.

GRAPE STUFFING

Peel and remove pips from enough grapes to fill the required number of pigeons.

PRUNE, ONION AND BACON STUFFING

1 handful soaked prunes, 1 medium sized onion, 3 rashers bacon, seasoning
Remove stones from prunes and chop roughly. Add chopped cooked onion,
but no liquid, and chopped bacon which has been lightly fried. Season.

INDEX